A Bushel's Worth
An Ecobiography

D0949385

Kayann Short

Torrey House Press, LLC

Salt Lake City • Torrey

First Torrey House Press Edition, August 2013
Copyright © 2013 by Kayann Short

Published by Torrey House Press, LLC
P.O. Box 750196
Torrey, Utah 84775 U.S.A.
www.torreyhouse.com

International Standard Book Number: 978-1-937226-19-0
Library of Congress Control Number: 2012955570

Cover design by Jeffrey Fuller, Shelfish • www.shelfish.weebly.com
Stonebridge Farm photographs by Kayann Short

A Sand County Almanac by Aldo Leopold (1949) 134w from "Good Oak." By permission of Oxford University Press, USA.

Brief quotes from pp. 54, 354 from BLACKBERRY WINE by JOANNE HARRIS. COPYRIGHT© 2000 BY JOANNE HARRIS. Reprinted by permission of HarperCollins Publisher.

For John, who cares what the harvest will bring.

Contents

A Bushel's Worth

On our farm vacations, each day was an adventure afforded by nature and our grandparents' hard work on the land.

A Trace of Rural Roots

In the rural economy of my childhood, everything had measure. After each meal at my grandparents' farm, plates were scraped into a pail and the remnants topped with milk. Once the dishes were done, my grandmother and I walked to the barnyard to empty the pail into a bowl outside the barn door for the mother cat and the kittens she hid in the hay. Half-wild, they wouldn't come out to eat until we returned to the farmhouse. Sometimes, glancing back, I'd catch a shimmer of quick cat fur as they darted under the door for their food. In this rural ritual, nothing—not the scraps left over from the table, not the steps to the barnyard and back—is wasted. Preserved even now by memory's spare prose, in that crossing a trace of happiness remains.

What do you take from a place you love and what do you leave behind? I was born in North Dakota, but my family left for Colorado when I was four. Every summer throughout my childhood, we would "go home" for our vacation to visit my two sets of grandparents on their farms. As soon as school was out each June, my family would make the long day's drive back in our station wagon, leaving before sunrise and stopping only for gas or a quick picnic lunch in a wind-blown park in Wyoming or South Dakota.

We were anxious to reach the Smith farm by early evening, where our cousins and aunts and uncles waited in the farm kitchen with our grandparents, watching out the big window facing the highway to see our dusty car turn down the gravel drive. After hugs and kisses in the farmyard, the adults went inside to ready our meal while Grandma led the children to the robin's nest hidden in the long grass near the house, its blue eggs mirroring the sky against the yellow prairie. We looked for that nest each year, a sign that we, like the robin, had returned.

After my grandmother's good supper, my sisters and brother and I would sit at the kitchen table long past our bedtime eating homemade toast with butter from my uncle's creamery or a late night bowl of sugary cereal, the kind we never had at home. As we watched the northern sunlight darken slowly over the prairie, we listened to the adults share last year's news until they noticed our dawdling and sent us to bed, even though the sun hadn't fully set. That far north, the twilight lingers much longer over the prairie than it does in the Colorado mountains. As the oldest, I was cross about going to bed while the sky was still light, so I watched the sun slowly disappear through the window of my grandmother's bedroom until it dropped behind the horizon and I dropped off to sleep. The farms meant robins' nests and long grass and the hot sun that didn't set until almost midnight, and I could hardly wait for school to end each year so we could go home again.

My parents had grown up on these farms and somehow the land and the rural lifestyle it supported seemed timeless. The farms provided a gathering place for our family and a playground for my cousins and siblings and me. Every day we would rush outside in the country air to hunt for the baby kittens in the barn, their newborn eyes still closed. Staying first at the Smith farm and then the Short, we would help our grandmothers gather eggs from the pecking chickens, watch our grandfathers milk cows, pick strawberries for shortcake, or ride in the hay wagon behind the tractor. Some summers, we stayed until the Fourth of July to set off fireworks, our grandfather keeping a watchful eye for the fire danger to the ripening fields. Each day was an adventure afforded by nature and our grandparents' hard work on the land.

When relatives visited on Sundays, dinner seemed to last all day. Fresh and home-canned vegetables from my grandparents' gardens always graced the table, along with fried chicken from one of the unlucky hens in the yard. Once, I even watched the proverbial chicken run around with her head cut off until she plopped over dead. My older cousin had warned me about the headless chicken, but she'd embellished a bit when she said the feet would run around by themselves when they were cut off, too. City kids didn't know these things, and I'd become a city kid, one who spent as much time indoors reading as outdoors playing. But I must have had some farm girl left in me because even after I discovered that my friends took real vacations to places like Disneyland, I still loved coming back every year to the farms.

Each summer, my sisters and brother and I searched for changes from our memories of visits before, yet were secretly relieved when the farms remained the same. Everything seemed just as it always had—each farm had its same cookie jar on the counter, the same games for us to play, the same grandparents awaiting our arrival. The barns were still the barns; the cats were still in the farmyard; the rusted Model T was still on the hill behind the sheds; and the sun still set long past the time we should have gone to bed.

As a child, I believed the farms would remain, season after season, waiting for my return. Now both farms have been sold, the farmhouses razed, and I haven't been back in years. But I still seek those memories in a landscape of grass and sun. Like my grandmother, I search for birds' nests, scanning trees for round weavings of sticks and scouting the meadow for soft mounds of plaited grass. When I'm lucky enough to find one abandoned, I bring it inside to place on a shelf with cream-colored pottery I've collected over the years. If the nest is small and downy, I protect it in a delicate French teacup in my china cabinet. If the nest is woven of small branches, I prop the whole limb against antique candlesticks. These are

3

Lerah, Myra, and the girl from town wading near the grassy bank of the wide creek.

A Trace of Rural Roots

the traces of my rural roots: natural things amongst the old, artifacts of living with grace and gratitude.

When I was in high school, I found an old sepia postcard in my grandfather's envelope of special photographs that he kept separate from family albums and treasured for reasons of his own. In this photograph from the 1910s, his older sisters Myra and Lerah pose with a woman identified only as "the girl from town" who my grandfather believed worked at the telephone company. The three young women are wading near the grassy bank of the wide creek, which is pronounced "crick" in that part of the country. Myra and Lerah, farm girls who didn't have many afternoons free to go wading, look a little surprised to find themselves standing barefoot next to each other in the water, holding up the skirts of their long dresses with both hands and giggling for the camera. Lerah, the youngest, beams playfully in her pretty white dress and hair bow, while Myra, the older sister who already worked hard on the farm, grins sheepishly in her wide-collared calico dress.

Turning slightly away from the sisters, the young woman from town is splashing through the water in a fancy white blouse, sleeves rolled to mid-arm, her long, crinoline skirt held above the water. Her eyes are closed, her smile wide, and her head thrown back in laughter. She was a town girl who probably didn't spend many afternoons wading in a cool summer creek. Town girls' lives were undoubtedly easier than those of farm girls, but a chance for an afternoon in the country with friends must have been a treat all the same.

Enchanted by this photograph, I made my grandmother write "Give this to Kayann Short" on the back. After my grandparents' deaths, my mother brought it home from North Dakota for me. In it, women's friendships form the meeting place of country and city. Against the backdrop of sky, creek, and prairie, the young women delight in each other's company and in the chance to move without restriction, breathe fresh air, touch the earth with bare feet, and gaze surrounded by the vastness stretching beyond them. The photo even captures the fine detail of long grass as it bends in the breeze, a sepia whisper behind the women's laughter.

This was a place I yearned for myself, yet which of the women I felt a kinship to was unclear, despite my bloodlines. I knew I descended from spirited women whose lives were made on the land. My great-great-grandmothers crossed oceans and prairies to raise families and crops on homesteads far from town. Great-grandma Short ran a dairy and, after my great-grandfather's death, a rooming house on her own. Great-aunt Myra harvested wheat behind hefty farm horses, their shoulders reaching above her head.

From my own grandmothers, I learned the strength and independence of rural ways, but, at seventeen, I was also drawn to the town girl delighting in the country, her fancy clothes less a hindrance as she wades in the creek than an embellishment to the prairie behind her. She had come from the city to visit my great-aunts on their farm, a working girl earning her own money, freer than her friends to do as she pleased. When she returned to sidewalks and streets, she would remember the coolness of the creek bottom. There's just more *outside* to life on a farm than "in town," as my grandparents would say. Looking at that photograph as a teenager, I didn't want to choose between town and country; somehow, I hoped my life could include both.

But growing up, I couldn't quite imagine that someday I would live on a farm of my own. I admired people—hippies, in 1960s and 70s terms—who went "back to the land" in an off-the-grid, *Mother Earth News* kind of way. But farms and farming seemed more remote, more isolated and secluded, than I thought I wanted to live.

When I went to graduate school in the 1980s, the national farm crisis underscored my reservations: farms like those of my grandparents were too big and too risky to provide a secure lifestyle. Owning a farm didn't seem practical, so my farm dreams would have to be of the past, not of the future.

Then I met John, who had a farm, and in the midst of a new agricultural movement called Community Supported Agriculture, my ideas about the viability of farming changed. Somehow, my farmroots had brought me back to the land, this time to a farming ecosystem that depended less on large-scale agricultural industry than on small-scale, local collaboration and community support.

As a young girl, I was a rock hound and my grandparents' farmyards were my stalking grounds. I scouted petrified wood, round picture agates, and red and gold siltstone flinted like arrowheads, bringing a pailful home to Colorado each summer to polish in my tumbler on the tool bench in our garage. For years, I kept a small dark brown stone, like magma from the earth's core cooled in the swirled shape of a horse's head and mane. My Grandma and Grandpa Smith's neighbor shared pieces of larger rocks he'd gathered on his own farm and from forays in that region. One was a polished oval picture agate, a horizon of shadowed trees landscaped across a champagne sky. Decades later, I had it edged in spiraled sterling with a silver chain, a memento in miniature of the land I'd left behind.

Now when I cross the bridge over the tree-lined irrigation ditch on the farm John and I own in the foothills of the Rocky Mountains, I trace the steps of my rural roots from my grandparents' farms and summers long ago. If my grandparents hadn't loved their land, I probably wouldn't be raising chickens and goats and growing flowers and herbs and vegetables on my own ten acres. I may have left North Dakota when I was young and only returned in the summers, but what I took with me was the belief that a life can be made on the land.

We can grow food, not only for ourselves, but for others. We can provide a place where people work within nature's cycles and reap its beautiful harvest. Once, my grandparents cultivated potatoes and wheat and a place for us to gather in season. Now John and I are the ones who watch the sunsets and seasons pass so that those we love have a farm to come home to.

Each day, we are the beneficiaries of *farmgiving*, the bound-less and bountiful generosity created by placing our lives alongside the land.

Dreams of Plenitude

"How about a few herbs for our salad? Do you like herbs?"
"Sure. Whatcha got?
"Let's walk out and see."

Years ago, when I first met John at the university where we both taught, I was delighted to learn he owned a farm. I had fond memories of summer vacations gathering eggs and playing with baby kittens in the hayloft at my grandparents' farms, so when John invited me for dinner at Stonebridge Farm to celebrate my birthday, I accepted. I would get to know more about John and I would get to spend time on a farm. Not a bad date.

The sun was still warm as John showed me around Stonebridge, a charming ten-acre farm outside of Boulder, Colorado. Tucked just off the Ute Highway that travels west into the St. Vrain Canyon of the Rocky Mountains, Stonebridge is lush with lofty willows and cottonwoods that line venerable irrigation ditches trisecting the land from north to south. As the farm's name suggests, a stone bridge arches across the lower Palmerton ditch that curves around the back of the house. Wooden bridges built from massive timbers span the middle ditch, named the Rough and Ready after the pair of brawny horses that plowed the steep banks, while the third, wider Highland ditch marks the eastern boundary of the property. With its 1911 farmhouse, weathervaned barn, and double-doored tractor shed, Stonebridge reminded me of my grandparents' farms in North Dakota, farms that even in my childhood felt like stepping back in time.

But on that late March evening I was thinking about the future, not the past. While dinner cooked, John and I walked out to the gardens to pick herbs—marjoram, chives, and tiny green onions—for an early spring salad. Touring the fields as the sun slanted behind the foothills, we looked for the hopeful tips of fall-planted garlic breaking through the moist soil. In another bed, newly emerging pea shoots whispered a season's promise, as if to say, "With care, something might grow here."

In the many years we've been together since that first visit, "walking out" has become a routine for John and me. "Do you want to walk out to the garden?" I'll ask. "I need some spinach for dinner."

"I'll walk out with you," John grins. Crossing the first wooden bridge by the flower garden, we listen for the splash of a startled muskrat diving toward its den in the muddy bank and note how high the ditch is running as the water, each drop owned and accounted for, rushes by. Taking our time, we scan the sky for red-tailed hawks while we chat about the day's events. We wander under the arching branches of the century-old cottonwood tree that leans alarmingly closer to the flower garden each year, and through the roses to note which are blooming. We pop a few raspberries in our mouths and pick a few more for dessert, and plot the next season's garden, all before we pick whatever vegetables we need for our evening's meal. On the way back to the house, we stroll across the farthest bridge near the herb garden, looping past the lush meadow and the sunny greenhouse before crossing the stone bridge back to the waiting kitchen. "Walking out" each day gives us a moment to catch up with each other as we ponder our future and plan the evening's homegrown meal.

Walking out, too, is part of living on the land. As we go through our days, we have chores to do, chickens to feed, gardens to water, and crops to gather, just as my grandparents did. As I cross and re-cross our ten acres, I think of my grandparents on their land—my grandmothers gathering eggs and tending their gardens, my grandfathers milking cows and working in the fields. When Henry David Thoreau wrote, "Half the walk is but retracing our steps," he could have been talking about farming, with its trips back and forth from house to field to house again. The steps I take each day also repeat my farming past. In walking out, I retrace my grandparents' steps with my own.

When John and I first met, we each had full lives with teen-aged daughters to raise and teaching careers at the local university. We joke that after we met, I got a tetanus shot and John bought a watch, acknowledgments of the changes necessitated by our pairing. Even that first meal together involved some negotiation of our differences: he had made pork chops and I am a vegetarian, something that had not come up in our coffee shop conversations. In this first of our culinary collaborations, he ate a second pork chop and I enjoyed the roasted potatoes, homemade bread, and salad with fresh herbs.

As we adapted in those early days to the rhythms and demands of each other's lives, the farm became our meeting place, not just as a geographical location, but as the site where our dreams could be joined and together fulfilled. The farm is now our home, but it is also much more. Each day, we are the beneficiaries of what I call *farmgiving*, the boundless and bountiful generosity created by placing our lives alongside the land. Farmgiving teaches us lessons about how to live with reciprocity in the natural world of which we are a part, drawn together by a sharing of gifts given freely and with love.

One of the lessons we have learned from farmgiving is to make the most of what we have. From abundance, we also learn thrift. If we waste what the earth so generously provides, we not only fail to appreciate those gifts, but we miss an opportunity to be generous with the earth's abundance. We need to think about what we can do with what we already have, whether it is a few vegetables that could create a delicious dinner, or a whole farm that could raise vegetables for many, many dinners.

Our farming friend says that the biggest crop we grow at Stonebridge is community. That's because, as a CSA, our farm grows for members who join the farm in the spring and receive a weekly share of the produce during the growing season, which for our farm is from the second Saturday of May until the last Saturday in October. Each share is held by a family, household, or group of members who collaborate on how those vegetables are used. Most of the members are subscribers who pay a fee at the beginning of the season, while others are barterers who exchange weekly labor in return for their share. Within CSA, people organize community around the desire for fresh produce, as well as a concern for food security in the form of local access to organic, non-genetically modified, and seasonal produce.

Although CSA seems to have several roots, the one from which we trace our farm started in Japan following the environmental and economic devastation of World War II. There, women consumers approached farmers to grow crops specifically and personally for them to ensure food safety and security. This concept is called *teikei*, meaning "putting a farmer's face on food." In this mutually beneficial arrangement, consumers share the risk of production by paying farmers at the beginning of the season and sharing the bounty or losses of the fields. Subscriber members share an interest in the farm that is social as well as financial because they have a personal stake in the survival of *their* farm. The *teikei* concept was given the name "Community Supported Agriculture" in this country by farmer Robyn Van En in 1985 at Indian Line Farm in Massachusetts.

In 1992, Stonebridge became the first Community Supported Agricultural farm in Boulder County when John, who was renting the farmhouse with his daughter, started the CSA with a farming partner of the farm's owners, an older couple who were retiring from farming. After a few years, they sold the farm to John and some partners, who later left to pursue their own endeavors. Soon John and I became co-owners of Stonebridge, and many seasons later, the CSA continues to thrive.

At Stonebridge, we like the idea of putting the farmers' faces on food since we believe people who know their farmers will support the farm each season, despite the ups and downs of farming. Stonebridge's slogan—"When the community feeds itself, the land and the people prosper"—means that not only does the community support local agriculture, but that the farm in turn helps create and support a community that cares about each other and the earth. Our subscribers pay their share in the early spring to help purchase the seeds and equipment we will need for that season. Other members barter their time and labor for their shares and take part in the decisions facing the farm each year. The relationship we are building in our community is a reciprocal one that challenges the anonymity of food systems today by placing those who eat food face to face with those who grow it.

While all CSAs are built on the idea that members share the bounty and the risks in variability and volume of crops each season, Stonebridge is a "share-the-harvest" CSA: instead of selling a portion of the crops to farmers' markets or grocery stores, all the food we produce is shared equally among members. Our members get first choice on what comes into the barn because it all goes to them, with the exception of bumper crop vegetables we sell to our friend's natural foods market in the small town nearby. Another way we're share-the-harvest is that we don't base the shares we give on the market value of each week's vegetables. In fact, we don't even keep track of weekly shares in a monetary way. Rather, we grow for abundance and divide the harvest each week between all the ninety shares of our farm. We prioritize our members and their vegetable needs and they appreciate the value they're getting for their subscription, while supporting the farm as well. With share-the-harvest, Stonebridge members know they're getting the best and the most that our farm has to offer.

Each spring, we love touring new subscribers around the farm on opening day and greeting our returning members in the barn. They tell us that just walking up the long driveway to our old, red barn feels like coming home. The air smells different here, they say, and they suddenly forget about the stresses of their daily lives. They like visiting the barn with its tables of bright vegetables to pick out their own rather than receive them in a box. Members have even told us that opening day is their favorite day of the year or that coming to the farm is the high point of their week.

We know that community supported agriculture is not going to replace industrial farming, but as fossil fuels become scarcer and food integrity is threatened, food production is one area where re-localization efforts can have an impact. By creating local markets for organically grown food, food dollars stay in a local economy, people eat healthier, fresher food, and pesticide and fossil fuel use are minimized. Amid these changes, CSAs can provide knowledge and practices on which to base future food policies. In this globalized economy of disappearing farmland and "Fast Food Nation" of diet-related health risks, CSA offers new ways, in the words of Joni Mitchell's iconic song, "to get ourselves back to the garden." Putting our faces on food allows us all to grow together through the seasons of our lives, renewing our friendships, shouldering our losses, and celebrating our accomplishments.

On a typical Saturday afternoon during the farm season, I'm hanging laundry on the line next to the house as members pick up their vegetable shares from the barn. I hear children jumping on the trampoline down by the bunkhouse and others laughing and tossing sticks into the creek with attentive parents watching nearby. I see a mom holding a curious toddler who is eagerly poking blades of grass through the hexagonal wire fence to the chickens scratching in the hen yard. Just past the greenhouse, a couple of middle-schoolers take turns hanging upside down on the swing that sweeps thrillingly over the creek. Earlier that day a teenaged girl volunteered with her mother picking spinach in the garden. As the children, like the crops, return to Stonebridge each spring, we remark on how tall they've grown over the winter, as one season yields to the next.

As far as we can ascertain, Stonebridge has been organic as long as it has been a farm. Stonebridge has had several owners since it was established in 1911 as a dairy farm, but all respected what the land offered and looked to natural methods of growing. We don't know all the details of Stonebridge's history, but we can tell from the careful maintenance of the original structures and preservation of spaces for wildlife in the meadow, woods, and ditches that previous owners farmed as stewards of the land.

Given the development pressure in our area, the fact that Stonebridge is still a farm and not a housing development or part of the nearby cement plant is somewhat miraculous. Instead, Stonebridge has been farmed for over one hundred years in much the same way. Despite technological innovations, the basic rhythm of farming has changed little over the last generations: crops still need to be planted with the seasons and the weather in mind, the fields need to be watered in the dry Colorado heat, and crops must be harvested before the soil freezes in winter.

John and I both come from farming backgrounds: his from working on farms in Oregon during summer breaks; mine from visiting my grandparents' farms in North Dakota each summer while I was growing up. Once I was on my own, I planted vast gardens, canned my own produce, and dried my own teas and herbs. Loving the feel of our hands in the soil gave us a head start on farming since we already knew a little about how food grows. Still, we both had more to learn from books and seed catalogs and magazines, other gardeners and farmers, and, mostly, from trial and error. We want to farm better, not just bigger, to meet the vegetable needs of our members as best we can in our summer-dry and winter-harsh climate.

One of Stonebridge's guiding principles is to keep our agricultural land in local production because just finding the land to farm on today is increasingly difficult. As Marion Nestle wrote in *Food Politics* in 2002, "In 1900, 40% of the [US] population lived on farms, but today no more than 2% do." In only two generations, families moved away from farming and farms, including my own parents, who couldn't wait to get off the farm to join the new, urban landscape of the post-war 1950s.

Stonebridge is not exactly a "family farm," at least not in the way we would traditionally think of that term. It has not been handed down to us from generation to generation, nor are we certain it will continue in the family after we are too old to farm anymore. We are not sure what will happen as we age, but we are committed to making sure the farm continues as a farm. We are hopeful that as people realize the benefits of growing food within their own communities, farms like ours may have a chance to continue for generations to come. For today, we will make the most of what we have by tending the land in the best ways we can.

"Are they ready yet?" Sweet red Jimmy Nardello peppers stuffed with Manchego cheese are roasting on the grill, one of the first delights of the pepper harvest. We saved these heirloom seeds from last year's crop, seeded them in April in our greenhouse, transplanted the young peppers in June, trellised them in July, and watered, weeded, and watched over them until the first August fruits glowed carnelian amid the emerald foliage. Our mouths were watering as we awaited the blend of sweet peppers and salty cheese in one bite, our anticipation months in the making. "Are they ready yet?" could have been asked, though, about any number of endeavors at Stonebridge, from building projects to community events to the harvest of a wide variety of vegetables, fruits, herbs, and flowers. On a farm, *we wait, we work, and the earth gives again.*

And because the land here at Stonebridge gives to us so generously, we can give in return. "I don't think I could share my farm like you do," a friend once remarked.

"But," I replied, "I don't think of it as just *my* farm." In fact, if I did, I would probably worry a lot more about getting everything done. I rarely refer to Stonebridge as "my farm." Instead, I think of it as "The Farm," because I know it has a life of its own beyond anything to do with me. John and I own the land, but it takes all of us—the barterers and interns who work with us, the subscribers who support us, and the friends and family who encourage us—to make this farm a viable, productive, and bountiful place for growing vegetables and community. Beyond that, the farm exists as a part of the natural world that shelters and nurtures us all. The land and the life that it harbors make this farm possible by giving us more than we will ever begin to know and more than could ever be tallied.

Farming is never easy. The relentlessness of the work and the unreliability of conditions can take their toll. Often, there is too much to do and not enough time to do it. Farming demands constant attention to some things within our control—what to plant and when and where to plant it—and many things that aren't—the availability of water and seeds, and weather, weather, weather. Each season starts with a variety of factors that farmers must weigh in their decisions but always with a flexibility to change when necessary. If one crop fails, plant again in hope of better conditions. Or try another variety, different field, more water, less water . . . or again next year.

It's all a gamble. Sometimes, even the tried and true doesn't work. Even with our combined farming experience to draw on, each season begins with questions that we do our best to answer and then stake our hard work toward ensuring we are right. Each season carries its own risks of drought that threatens the fields, of machinery that might break, and of injuries that prevent the physical labor demanded each day. The worry of accident is constant in a life that includes tractors, chainsaws, old buildings, and heavy lifting. We've both made trips to urgent care for tetanus boosters and stitches with farm injuries like smashed fingers and rusty nail punctures. "Safety first," we remind each other as we go out to work, meaning take necessary precautions, ask for help when needed, and keep our eyes and ears attuned to each other in the fields.

Relationships are not easy either, and John and I have had our bumps along the way. That first fall together amid stresses of work and family as I drove back and forth from town to the farm, I wondered whether I would be around to reap the garlic we were planting in October in anticipation of a spring harvest. I wasn't sure that this farm could be my farm too. When the flower garden I planted outside the irrigation pattern dried up and died without me there to water it, I felt discouraged. I didn't know yet whether I could fit my life into the cycles of the farm or whether my dreams could be joined on one piece of land with John's. We were both so busy with our daughters and our jobs that finding time to spend together, let alone farm, looked unlikely. Making a commitment to something as simple as garlic seemed a risk I wasn't sure I wanted to take.

But like relationships, fall crops demand faith. You cannot see their growth until the earth warms again. As John and I placed each clove in the dimpled field, we hoped that, like the garlic, our love would send down roots to nourish and protect it through the cold, dark winter. If we could imagine a time when new shoots would emerge, perhaps the winter wouldn't be so long.

Promisingly, the garlic did come up in the spring, and John and I made it through the dark winter as well. With each day, we discovered that farming was the perfect way to spend time together. We renovated the farmhouse so that each would be comfortable there. With a sledge hammer and a pry bar, we tore down old walls to open the rooms to light and make a larger space for meals with family and friends. We planted a new flower garden where the irrigation system could reach and we planned projects that combined our interests at the farm. Working day by day, we began to see how we could join our lives on the farm.

One June day, John and I walked hand in hand over the wooden bridge of the irrigation ditch as a muskrat paddled by. In the flower garden we had planted together, he in his handwoven shirt and I in my grandmother's navy blue wedding dress, we promised our commitment to each other and to the land on which we stood. As a cousin strayed close to the bank of the Highland ditch that marks the east edge of the farm, our minister friend Priscilla Inkpen reminded guests that nature offers its own kinds of gifts: in this case, poison ivy. We laughed with friends and family gathered in the old apple orchard to celebrate our vows as a few drops of rain fell, blessings from the land that would now encircle our lives.

Under the canopy of the leaning cottonwood tree, John and I listened closely as our musician friend Coyote Joe sang "The Stonebridge Wedding Song." The lyrics he wrote then still ring true:

There'll be toil, and sweat by your brow
But the challenges you'll answer somehow
And through it all you'll grow stronger
And closer on this land.

None of it—the crops, the friendships, the community, and the deep love and respect we have for each other—will come without hard work, but by walking out to the garden together, season after season, we hope to reap a harvest beyond our wildest imaginings.

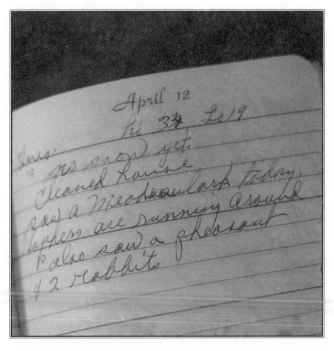

In her diaries, my grandmother would note signs of the seasons changing.

Marking Her Days With Grace

In my Grandma Smith's diaries, each sparse entry starts with a weather report. A true farmer, she always recorded the weather, both the high and low temperatures and noteworthy conditions like sheer wind or a blinding snowstorm. Farmers depend on the weather, so marking its changes helped her remember the years, but in rural North Dakota, the weather meant something more: it determined the possibilities of each moment and the strength needed to endure the extremes of life on the prairie.

Some days in July, she would just write "Hot."

Another series of weather entries in 1966 reads like a poem:

Wed, March 9: 45 degrees above
snow melting
just like spring
Thurs, March 10: No need for a weather report.
Fri, March 11: Weather is fine.

My favorite weather entry reads: *Sat, Jan 29, 1966: This morning it's 40 below so won't be very warm today.* Even in a North Dakota winter, that could be considered an understatement.

In my grandmother's make-do world, "Won't be very warm" means "Won't be going anywhere today." My grandparents lived in the country, so snowstorms meant no trips to town and no visitors dropping by until the weather cleared. I can imagine my grandmother watching the wide winter-gray sky from the kitchen windows while she baked her weekly loaves of bread. She was a slim woman who in her later years never seemed to get warm. For her last Christmas, we gave her a heavy Scandinavian sweater to take away the chill. After she died, I inherited the sweater but I've never worn it; I don't want to lose the smell of her face powder lingering in the thick wool.

Winter in North Dakota is unforgiving. An incautious mistake—an empty fuel tank, bad tires, turning down the wrong dirt road—can mean death in a blizzard that shrouds the prairie in icy white. And winter stays into spring there, as my grandmother's diary confirms.

Fri March 4, 1966: 12 degrees above hi for today. It's nice here today but not so warm. Is close to zero. We were lucky to miss being in the storm the last three days. Some lives lost in S. Dakota. I baked a pie.

Here and on the next page, my grandmother tucked two newspaper clippings about the days-old storm. "Snows Wrath on Our Path" warns one. "Holy Cow! No Snowplow!" exclaims the second.

Luckily, my grandparents missed that blizzard and got to town so my cousin could try on the dress of "tissue gingham" our grandmother had been sewing for her. But, my grandmother admits again in her understated way, "The wind was so howling, I didn't like it." With those words, I can see her watching the sky for snow and waiting for the roads to clear so that she could venture into town to visit family and buy supplies, perhaps even some fabric for my Easter dress in Colorado.

Rereading my Grandma Smith's diaries, I look for clues about how she spent her days. She sewed continually and she baked a lot of bread—six or seven loaves at a time. She kept her flour in a deep pullout bin in the kitchen cabinet that held a fifty-pound bag. She would bake once a week, making enough for morning toast, noon sandwiches, and evening bread and butter. Covered by thin cotton dishtowels embroidered with vegetable people or sunbonnet girls, her loaves rose high in their pans.

Sometimes she would make cinnamon rolls along with the bread, letting the grandchildren roll out the rectangle of dough and spread it with real butter from our uncle's creamery. Then we would spoon on brown sugar and sprinkle the dough with cinnamon, roll it up tight, pinch the seam, slice it into a dozen thick rounds, and pack them carefully in the cake pan to rise. Fresh and hot from the oven, the sugar- and butter-filled rolls melted on our fingers and tongues. No "store-boughten" cinnamon rolls could ever taste as good.

Grandma Smith worked hard on the farm, even after she and my grandfather weren't raising animals and crops anymore. A typical entry of her busy life reads:

Tues, Feb 11, 1966:
I baked 2 apple pies
put in freezer
scrubbed the kitchen floor
fed the cats at the barn
burned the paper
this pm I'm going out visiting.

I remember my grandmother down on her hands and knees scrubbing the floor in case someone stopped by. I marveled that she wore dresses around the house with her old pantyhose, not wanting to waste a brand new pair. When I asked her why she didn't just go barelegged, she exclaimed in disapproval, "No, I can't do *that!*" She was fashionable her entire life, even when scrubbing the floor.

Because the Smith farm was on the highway into Williston, the county seat, many of my grandparents' farming friends and relatives would stop by unannounced for coffee on their way to or from town. In her diaries, Grandma Smith noted who had visited that day and what she had baked—lemon meringue pie, angel food cake, or a kind of date cookie she called "Matrimonial Chews." Visitors were so common at the farm that one entry comments on *not* receiving guests: *Sat, March 9, 1985: I was home all day. Baked a pie but no company.*

My grandmother rarely noted her feelings or reflections about her life, but one of the few reflective passages she wrote makes me laugh: *Tues, Jan 25, 1966: I'm cleaning the basement—and it sure looks better.* That "sure" sounds just like her, a mix of practicality and positive thinking. If you're going to do something, it seems to say, do it right—and be happy you've done it.

Why weren't her diaries more personal, more revealing of her thoughts and feelings? I don't think she worried about someone discovering them. After her death, we found these few diaries stuck in an old cabinet in the basement, more tucked away for safekeeping than hidden. I think instead that she didn't feel a need to express personal feelings in diary form. What was important was recording the everyday events of her life, keeping track of the weather and the visitors, the comings and goings of a farm on the edge of town.

In a few entries, though, I catch a glimpse of a more private side of my grandmother, moments of the solace she found in the natural world. In her diaries, she would note signs of the seasons changing, especially when a long, cold winter was turning away for spring:

Wed, April 6, 1983: We walked to the creek and found mayflowers and heard a meadowlark sing.

Tues, April 12, 1983: No snow yet. Cleaned house. Saw a meadowlark today. Gophers are running around and also saw a pheasant and two rabbits.

In entries like these, I imagine her looking out the window over the prairie, although "prairie" is my word, not hers. She would say "pasture," since the long grass is where my grandparents grazed their cattle. I picture her walking to the creek to look for mayflowers, grateful for a sign that spring had finally made its way to the north. She paid attention to the creatures around her because they inhabited the same piece of land. She marked her days by the weather and the seasons because they formed the backdrop of her life on the farm, determining each day's possibilities. These diary entries reveal an intimacy with nature that seems a private part of my grandmother's life, quiet moments of grace in the midst of her busy days.

In North Dakota, the monotony of the prairie is broken only where the horizon yields corn or wheat or sunflowers. Trees only grow along rivers and creeks or in long-rowed breaks planted to protect farmhouses from the fierce Canadian wind. Against the prairie's cornsilk-green and yellow chaff, my grandmother planted flowers in blazing swathes emboldening the landscape from the country roads running east of the farm. My grandmother grew what she called "the front row flowers"—gladiolas, sweet peas, zinnias, and poppies—in front of the steps along the highway-facing side of the farmhouse and in crocks on the outdoor steps. Whenever she watered her flowers, a few drops would leak from the spigot onto the mint that grew in a metal ring underneath. Because water was in such short supply, keeping a little mint alive in the ominous North Dakota heat was my grandmother's way of beating the prairie.

When I turned fifty, my mother sent me a black and white photo of myself as a baby in my grandmother's lap on those very steps. In the picture, I'm not looking at the camera; instead, I'm reaching for the pinwheel petunias in the old flowerpot sitting next to me, too tempting not to touch.

Reaching for the flower is one of my grandmother's legacies to me. Planting the gladiola bulbs as soon as the ground can be worked each spring on my own farm, I think of my grandmother and her persistent attempts to stand out against the prairie. When I dig up the bulbs in fall's slanting light to store over the winter, I think again of her hard work baking bread, butchering chickens, and putting by all the food her family would need.

But the real hardship for my grandmother, I think, was the isolation of her rural life, especially in the long winters. No wonder she baked every day in the happy chance that someone would visit. No wonder her diary celebrates the first mayflowers and meadowlark call of the spring.

The 2006 Snowstice blanketed the barn and old truck.

Snowstice

On December 26, the light at the end of the day slants warmly across the window seat where I'm mending. After the hectic pace of harvest and holidays, I finally have a quiet moment in the day's waning sunshine for smaller tasks set aside for the farm season's end. In winter, I gravitate to this upstairs window like a sunflower tracking the sun. From the south, the light is brighter here than anywhere else in the house as the sun peers straight in through barren treetops.

We have just passed the solstice, the turnaround time of midwinter when the sun is at its greatest angular distance from the earth's tilt. "Solstice" comes from the Latin words *sol* (sun) and *sistere* (to stand still). For about three weeks before the winter solstice, which in the Northern Hemisphere is between December 20 and 22, the sun sets at nearly the same time each evening; the same is true for sunrises following the solstice. This stasis feels like the earth is stuck in space because the daylight doesn't seem to change. While the solstice day itself is the shortest day of the year, at our latitude the earliest sunset occurs two weeks before the solstice and the earliest sunrise two weeks after. On Colorado's Front Range of the Rocky Mountains, the sunset is always precipitous—one moment bright, the next dim—but somehow today seems already a bit longer than yesterday as the last rays of light drop obliquely behind the snowy peaks and the frigid night begins.

I call the winter solstice the "snowstice" after the December 20 blizzard of 2006 that suddenly dropped two to three feet of snow in Denver, the Eastern Plains, and the Front Range

31

where we live. By most accounts, the snowstice storm was the fourth largest recorded in Colorado history, remarkable even in a state known for its snow. In a blizzard like that, cars hang together like children holding hands in a prairie storm that blows in unexpectedly during the school day, sending families home in a mittened string of oldest to youngest, praying to hit a house or barn rather than wander lost on the prairie. There is no stopping on a darkened snow-driven road, only eyeing the intermittent light of reflectors posted along the shoulder and hoping the tracks in front of you lead to safety.

But after a storm, the sun is brighter than on any other morning as sparkling ice crystals refract the brilliant glare, making winter the perfect time to look at familiar surroundings in a new light. After a snowstorm, I walk the farm, silent on the fresh snow. Tracks left by scurrying rabbits and squirrels cross my path. I spot red-tailed hawks with their snowy plumage and bald eagles perched regally in the bare willows off the creek. Once, I witnessed a coyote stalking a small rodent—a vole or a mouse—on the top of a snowdrift, the predator so intent on its prey that it did not sense my approach. I watched as it tensed, leaped, and captured the animal in its jaws. Only then did it see me; we had surprised each other, thinking we were the only large creatures about on that snowy day.

In winter, we think in black and white, shadows and light, the contrasts stark against a graying sky as fresh snow hoods the upper sides of the tree limbs, white flocking on dark branches. The lengthening shadows of tree limbs across the snow form elegant etchings that capture the frigid outlines of winter's stately demise. When the sun sits low on the horizon and nothing grows in the frozen soil, the earth itself seems barren. Life is more fragile in this bleak midwinter—tiny creatures scurrying across the bright snow are vulnerable to predators, their dark bodies profiled against the blank winter canvas. Our lives, too, are made of a fragile thing; the line between life and death is sharper in winter, when walking out to get the mail without a jacket risks a numbing chill that hurries us back indoors to the waiting woodstove.

On the first day of the new year, John and I walked in the waning sunlight as snowflakes fell gently on the farm. I scanned the trees for abandoned nests, the fledglings flown long ago; the week before I had found an oriole nest, like a felted mitten, blown down from the branch where it had hung. Crossing the bridge of the middle ditch, we surprised a red-tailed hawk in the boughs of an old cottonwood, then five minutes later were surprised ourselves by a bald eagle flying south and then east in the graying twilight. Walking with the goats to check the dwarf plum and apple trees, we saw an owl land in a tree along the ditch, taking off low from the branch minutes later. As we turned the goats into their shed for the night, we could hear the owl's hooting through the soft, snowy evening, answered by geese in a long line heading south. We brought in armfuls of wood to warm the kitchen and living room for a quiet evening, a promising beginning to the new year together.

A week later, I'm working in my study when I hear the pair of great-horned owls that have graced the farm for years calling in the trees to the east of the driveway. They're close, so I throw on a jacket and tall boots to run outside in the snowy dusk. With just enough light to see, I follow their calls, one deeper, one higher in response, to the tall pine trees off the parking lot in front of the house. But by the time I reach the trees, the pair has moved to the other side of the ditch, so I walk up the driveway and head into the thicket of overgrown elms and pines between our farm and the neighbor's.

It's quiet now, but I keep walking in the silent woods. Suddenly, I hear one owl hooting nearby, so I start up the bank toward the higher ditch. I wait, but when I don't see an owl silhouetted against the rising moon, I scramble back to the path. I try to walk softly, but the snowdrifts are stiff and I crash through with a crusty crunch. When I come to a place where the bushes have grown across the path, I part the branches with my hands to step through—and I'm facing an owl in the crux of a branch just ten feet in front of me. The owl is scanning the forest, moving its great-horned head from side to side like a lighthouse beacon. It perches sphinx-line on the pine's lowest branch, its head thrust slightly in front of its body. I've never been this close to an owl before, close enough to see its white face and brown markings.

I try not to move, but the owl sees me anyway. The vast head stops rotating and the eyes stare without alarm, noting my presence with feigned curiosity. "Hello, Owl," I whisper softly. We stare at each other for a few seconds until its mate calls from the other side of the creek. My owl lifts its wings like a cape, pushes off from the branch, and flaps just enough to glide through the trees. I glimpse its golden underside, and then, it's gone. As I turn and walk back through the snow to the warmth of the house, the owls, reunited, call behind me.

In winter, we look for any reminder of summer's glow. Dried grasses caught mid-wave in the snow's fall stand yellow against the glaring white: frozen rays of sunshine left over from a summer warmth. Long and curving against the snow, they ripple beach-like, the whiteness of the snow like sand on the shore in Virginia Woolf's *To the Lighthouse*: ". . . and on the right, as far as the eye could see, fading and falling, in soft low pleats, the green sand dunes with the wild flowing grasses on them, which always seemed to be running away into some moon country, uninhabited of men." Winter's yearning for summer warms us, like a candle's flame promises a campfire's glow, but it's still winter and the light is still as well.

From winter, I've learned the lesson of resting and all the "re-" words that go with it: rebirth, renewal, restore, renovate, regenerate, and, most of all, reflect. Winter is a time at Stonebridge when both the land and the farmers rest. The land sleeps under a coat of white. Small mice and voles tunnel under the snow for harvest remains; red-tailed hawks with their snowy breasts survey the fields for any movement that portends dinner. Inside the house, we knit, spin, write, and catch up on our sleep. We pile thick quilts and down comforters on the beds and wait for our own heat to thaw the flannel sheets. We warm our insides with tea brewed from farm herbs and thick stews simmered from the vegetables stored last fall in the freezer, pantry, and root cellar. Mostly, winter is a time to rest from social obligations and the busyness of our lives so we can slow down and take stock of all we have accomplished. The winter wipes clean the slate of last year's misgivings, knowing spring will offer us a new chance to re-write our dreams. In the quiet of the farmhouse, we plan again, grateful for another season of farmgiving on its way.

Tonight we walked outside at dusk to find the full January moon, called the Winter Moon by colonial Americans, the Wolf Moon by some Native tribes, and the Old Moon in England, rising over the tree line as something hooted in the cottonwood outside the house. Backlit by the moon, a great-horned owl perched in the leafless cottonwood on a branch high above the garage. But then, the call came again from further away, so we searched the horizon to the south. There, on the transformer tip of an electrical pole, balanced a smaller great-horned, its cat-like ears silhouetted against the twilight. We stood under the first owl and hooted in reply, hoping to see it take flight, but it only stared back unflinchingly with its great round eyes. Finally, the second owl flapped off the pole, across the yard, and over the tall trees to the east. Ignoring our calls, the first owl soon followed in the lunar light and the night was still again.

In winter, it is light we crave as much as warmth. Living according to nature's rhythms provokes us in winter with cold and snow, icy roads, dark days, and long nights. Wool-wrapped and woodstove-huddled, we must look deeper to find winter's gifts of solitude and rest while we yearn for warmer times. In the last, lingering rays of the solstice sun descending over the blue shadowed foothills of the Rockies, the long snowstice shadows throw a mantle of stillness over the land, as if the world has slowed for a time, like the solstice sun stuck in its rise and set until the earth's insistent circling sets it free again.

A Bushel's Worth

In early spring, flats of seeds germinate quickly in the warm
greenhouse.

38

Starts

Nature does not hurry, yet everything is accomplished.
—Lao Tzu

The first workday with the bartering crew at Stonebridge Farm falls in early spring with snow almost invariably on the ground. But this year the day is uncharacteristically sunny, although the mountains had threatened to send snow our way the day before. We need moisture, but the warmth is welcome too on this first day as we set the new farm season in motion. Here we are again, ready to make soil and plant seeds and clean the winter-deadened debris from the land.

Before we get to work, we gather around the woodstove in the Sunflower Community Room with cups of tea and coffee, saying hello after a winter's absence and sharing stories after four months of Saturdays not spent in the garden together. Sometimes a new baby, new job, travel overseas, or, sadly, the death of a loved one, have brought us to an altered phase of our lives, yet the farm and its cycles of care mark a continuity for all of us. Because Stonebridge is a community supported agricultural farm, we like to say we emphasize the "C" in "CSA" since the work we do here is as much about people as produce.

Spring at Stonebridge wasn't always such a joyous return. In earlier years of the CSA, the fall fields were often left unturned and no cover crops were sown to prepare the soil for the next spring's planting, as if the farmers had thrown down their tools one autumn day and wandered off for warmer climates. In those earlier times, before the barterers provided stability for the farm, the strain of finishing the season was so great, no one could imagine doing it again just a few months later. With full-time jobs outside of the farm, John and I couldn't do all the work ourselves after the partners we'd had along the way left for jobs or farms of their own. We knew that we wanted to keep the community focus of Stonebridge, rather than market our produce off the farm, so we turned to that community for help.

In 2000, John and I initiated a bartering structure at Stonebridge that asked a handful of members to exchange farm work for their seasonal share of vegetables. We had read about bartering at Indian Line Farm in Massachusetts, the first CSA in the United States, and it seemed to us the perfect way to build the social structure of the farm. To our surprise and delight, some exceptional people took us up on the offer and the bartering crew began. The barterers work four hours a week for eight months a year, from March through October, in exchange for their share of vegetables, starting two months before the official CSA season begins. Now a community has formed around the work, and, come mid-March, everyone is excited to farm together once more.

Hands and hearts warmed by fire and friends, we turn to the morning's tasks. After we list the possibilities—some folks can do this, other folks can do that—one seven-year-old "barterer" adds, "And some people can climb the big tree over the ditch!" Chores chosen, we finish our last sips of coffee and head out in groups to begin the new season's work of waking up the farm in the spring sunshine.

With the bright white peaks of the mountains to the west reassuring us that we will again have water to irrigate the fields, some of us set up a seed-starting assembly line in the cozy greenhouse. While Sarah, Andy, Mike, and Jenny make the mixture we use for starts by combining peat, sand, compost, and soil dug from the fields, Jay, Michelle, and Joe make blocks with a tool that compresses the moistened mix into four cubes that look like chocolate brownies with dimples on top to hold the seed. Last but not least in our assembly line, Julie, Eva, and Deirdre drop and cover the seeds in the dimples of the newly blocked flats.

Since we've already seeded the alliums in February, the earliest plants for the bartering crew to start each spring are the brassicas: cauliflower, broccoli, kohlrabi, and cabbages. As we work, we can't help but sing a line from our friend Coyote Joe's song, "The Things You Do": *Kohlrabi just tastes a little bit funny.* And it is funny-looking, like a round spaceship with antennaed leaves sprouting from its dome. Together, we fill 38 flats with 50 blocks per flat: 1900 new plants that will be transplanted when the weather warms. Before too many weeks have passed, flats will fill every nook and cranny, shelf and ledge, of the entire greenhouse. With our hands in the soil, we gain a first work morning's satisfaction of creating nice, neat rows of starts that will provide food for us later in the season.

While some barterers get seeds started in the greenhouse, others work outside in the spring air. The "Garlic Apostles"— Peter, Paul, and Timothy—took a vow years ago to keep the garlic beds weed-free, so this first day they pull the hay mulch back from the shoots to open the field to sun and assess the garlic's growth since planting it last fall. It's a little slow to emerge this year after such a cold winter, the green tips just starting to poke through the soil. Some of the soft-necked bulbs will be harvested in early June for green garlic, while the hard-necked varieties will send up curly scapes, thick middle shoots that carry the plants' seed heads, which we'll harvest in mid-June.

Scapes are one of the farm's surprises: we didn't figure out for many years that they can be pulled from the center of the plant and used in recipes instead of garlic cloves. Equally important, after the scape is removed, the plant then puts energy into larger bulbs below rather than into flowers at the tip of the scape's curl. The barterers love to harvest the scapes as they compete to pull the longest scape straight out of the stalk with a pop before it breaks off. While the children make scape bracelets by curling them around their wrists, the adults cry, "Look at this one!" when they harvest one they think is the longest. Scapes are an extra gift from an already generous plant—we pick hundreds of them each June.

While some barterers have adopted the garlic, others have embraced the raspberries, which need yearly attention in our perennially grassy plots. Headed by Jan, our raspberry expert, the raspberry crew not only weeds, but prunes the old canes in anticipation of summer fruit. On that first cool spring day, in gloves and coats, Lisa, Emily, and Lindsay make another valiant attempt to clear the plot of the rhizome grass whose roots crisscross the entire farm.

March in Colorado is still intermittently winter; we get our heaviest snows this month, sometimes even into April. A spring snow is wetter than a snow in December or January; it's the snow that ensures the mountains' snowpack and readies our soil for the season. Our first gathering in March is usually snowy, but if the ground is clear of snow, some folks spend the morning raking the ubiquitous sticks scattered across the farm by winter winds. With three irrigation ditches running through our land, Stonebridge is thick in towering willows and cottonwoods that grow along the banks. Kunga and the two Amys fill wheelbarrows full of sticks to dump on the burn pile for a spring bonfire, and as they rake, they find new green grass stretching its blades toward the sun.

Before we know it, noon arrives and the first bartering day is done. We've achieved much this spring morning: flats of seeds will soon germinate in the warm greenhouse, garlic and raspberry beds are ready for new growth, and the farm has been tidied for another season. More planting, weeding, and watering must be done if we want fresh vegetables this season, but together, the work will be accomplished. Today we have found again the rhythm of the farm, a rhythm that does not hurry but reminds us why we do what we do here at Stonebridge.

In April, there's mud. Mud cakes our boots as we work in the rain to ready the farm for the members' first pick-up day in May. We clean the barn, cup up more tomatoes and peppers that were seeded in flats a few weeks earlier, and weed the bluehouse—so called to differentiate it from the greenhouse—where lettuces are slow to grow in the cold weather. Mud is everywhere. Paul carts wheelbarrows full of wood chips to spread in front of the entrances to the greenhouse and barn. The raspberry weeders kneel in mud and when we gather in the Sunflower Room after our morning's work, everyone's boots drag mud onto the (mostly) clean floor. April showers bring . . . mud, a part of spring I'm always happy to see pass.

The greenhouse toad came back at the end of April. We first spotted her on the last Sunday of the month, but we suspected her presence for a week before that from the toad-shaped imprint in the muddy spot between the water irises growing in a bucket in our greenhouse pond. We call it the toad throne because she likes to perch there above her kingdom of floating water lilies. Soon she was joined by another Woodhouse toad and, a couple weeks later, we found three baby toads in the pond as well. Each spring I look for toads in the greenhouse. They seem a lucky omen, a sure sign that spring is finally here.

One spring brought another auspicious pair of creatures to Stonebridge. In April, our daughters and son-in-law were at the farm to plant a Black Walnut tree in memory of John's dad, Noel Martin, who died the Christmas before. As we walked toward the north end of the farm with our shovels and buckets of compost, I noticed wooly owl pellets on the ground under a cottonwood tree that towers over the garden. I scuffed the pellets with the toe of my shoe to find the skeletal remains of mice and voles and birds. Realizing that the pellets marked the presence of the pair of great-horned owls that have lived at the farm for many years, I looked up into the tree to spot a large owl nest of leaves in the crook of the towering limb. "Look, an owl nest," I announced, pointing to the tree, but it didn't occur to me that "nest" might mean "babies," because we'd never seen any on the farm before.

A few days later, I was showing the nest to the Thursday morning bartering crew when suddenly we realized a baby owl was on the branch next to the nest—and then another came into view. Less than a foot tall, they were so still, like outcrops of the limb itself, that it took a moment to realize they weren't made of bark, but rather feathers, fuzzy like a puppy's fur, the owlets' great round eyes staring at us without movement. As their mother watched protectively nearby, we left them alone and quietly picked spinach in the shade of their nested branch. I came out later to snap a few photos of the babies, hoping I wouldn't disturb them, but unwilling not to document such astounding creatures. I knew that once grown, their parents would drive them off the farm in search of their own food, but for now, they seemed content to venture further up the tree.

Before the subscription season officially starts the second Saturday in May, the barterers plant two big crops on our early spring Saturdays: alliums and brassicas. It takes the whole crew to transplant these crops from the starts in the greenhouse. Planting in the early spring isn't easy because we're not in farming shape yet—especially our knees as we bend and stoop to tuck the plants into the ground. Since most of us are decidedly middle-aged, we joke that in a couple years we'll be making the dimples that mark our planting spots with our walkers instead of with the tractor.

In the early part of the season, getting started on Saturday mornings is a little like revving up an old engine after a sub-zero night. It takes a few turns of the crank before the gas is flowing again. As if coming out of hibernation, everyone moves slowly in a haze of deliberation, contemplating the work to come. The younger barterers arrive with coffee cups in hand; we all agree we're not officially awake until the caffeine has kicked in and our bodies have adjusted to the sharp morning air. Kneeling next to each other in the cold fields, the conversation doesn't start until we shake ourselves awake enough to ask, "What'd you do this week? How are the kids? How's your shoulder/back/ankle?"

Eventually our muscles loosen and the chatter spills across the bed of tiny onions as we squat, plant, and scoot. We discuss roads not taken, our plans for the summer, money worries, and health. And then, because we're getting close to lunchtime, the talk turns to the vegetables we're growing and what delicious dishes we'll make from them. As we warm up to the work, the spring sunshine, and the soil that's perfect for planting, we're thrilled to see such a huge job accomplished in a single morning. We've planted 8,000 alliums—several varieties each of leeks and onions, each as tiny as a new blade of grass.

A couple Saturdays later, we transplant the next big crop, the brassicas—broccoli, cauliflower, cabbage, and kohlrabi. Since these are shorter-season vegetables, we plant fewer brassica starts than alliums, so transplanting goes more quickly, but they need the added step of covering with gauzy row cover to guard them from flea beetles, the garden's earliest pest. We finish in record time and stand back to survey the fields full of plants we'll begin to harvest in a few weeks. Now all the transplanting is done until early June when the tomatoes, peppers, eggplant, and basil go out to the fields, accompanied by the marigolds that help repel undesirable insects and attract the desirable ones. The Thursday crew has already transplanted the annual herbs—dill, cilantro, parsley, and chervil—that we started in the greenhouse this year to beat the weeds rather than seeding directly into the fields.

On opening day, rain was predicted but the sun rises strong and clear. Picking vegetables on opening day follows the same routine every year. After we stand around a few minutes saying good morning and "Here we go!", we load bikes and bike trailers for transporting vegetables from the fields to the barn with multi-colored plastic picking baskets called *trugs* and the tools we'll need for harvesting: forks for digging Jerusalem artichokes and a pocketed bucket with the *horis*—Japanese digging tools—and clippers.

We start the morning by observing the owl twins and their mom, who has flown off into the trees across the field, perhaps to lead us off the trail from the babies. Then we dig green garlic bulbs that have "volunteered" by planting themselves in last fall's garden and pick spinach, taking the biggest leaves from the fall-planted bed. Picking spinach elicits our yearly debate: should it be picked quickly, pulling the leaves by the handful, or slowly and deliberately, picking each leaf individually? As always, we say, "Pick it how you'd like to eat it," so eventually the more discerning manner wins. However it's picked, all Stonebridge spinach is a delicacy this time of year, sweet, crisp, and very, very green. Spinach is the reason we start our season earlier than other CSAs in our area—it grows well this close to the foothills. Many of our members say they don't care if we give anything else on opening day. After a long winter, they're ready for spinach, and lots of it.

As the trugs are filled, the veggies are biked into the barn by the intrepid bikers with a trailer hitched to the back. We used to truck in the produce, but, years ago, decided bicycles were safer and more ecological for trips between field and barn, and the vegetables stay fresher because they're transported more quickly. Sometimes, though, we get a little ambitious about how much a trailer can hold. You can always tell when a rider has taken the corner on the downhill side of the bridge too quickly from the spinach left in the middle of the road. Walking back to check on the progress in the barn, I follow a Hansel and Gretel trail of spinach leaves, gathering as I go. Spring spinach is so sweet and delicious, I hate to waste a single leaf.

After we finish harvesting the spinach, we dig the walking onions, pungent enough to scent the whole barn, and all the Jerusalem artichokes we can find. We like them sliced and fried in olive oil with a touch of butter, like the "fresh-fried" potatoes my mom makes, a special treat because they demand constant attention to brown without burning. One of our first shared Stonebridge recipes was Jerusalem Artichoke Soup, a response to our members asking, "What do we do with this?" It's still an early spring favorite among our longest-standing members.

We finish up the pick with rhubarb, harvesting the red stems and slicing off the huge leaves, which shouldn't be eaten because they contain toxins. This year the crop is a little sparse, but we give enough for a small rhubarb crisp and we'll pick more in a couple weeks. Maybe the cold, dry winter affected the size and quantity of the rhubarb. Who knows? What we do know is that the same conditions aren't favorable for every crop. If the spring is cool and long, the broccoli will be happy, but the tomatoes and peppers will be transplanted late. If the spring is short and hot, we can transplant those crops earlier, but the fall-planted spinach will go to seed not long after the season begins. Today we are giving beautiful spinach, walking onions, Jerusalem artichokes, rhubarb, and gourds we dried over the winter. Most years, radishes, lettuce, and Asian greens join the list; with this year's cool spring, they're on their way. In just two weeks, we'll give twice that variety of vegetables, and by August, three times that again, but for this first pick, the real share is a welcome to another season at Stonebridge.

By ten o'clock, we shed our sweatshirts and are soon down to our shirtsleeves. With the pick biked in for our barn boss, Eva, to count, weigh, and arrange in the barn, we weed the strawberries and the rose garden until it is time to meet the new members at eleven o'clock by the barn. John gives his annual safety talk: be careful near the ditches, stay with your children at all times, don't play on the equipment, watch for "leaves of three, let them be" poison ivy. Following his talk, I lead the tour to familiarize new members with the fields and the layout of the farm. As we walk out toward the largest field, I don't intend to mention the new owls because I'm concerned that a large group of people might frighten the mother into abandoning the babies, but someone spots some barterers pointing at the nest in the tree, so the owlets become the stars of the tour after all. I'm secretly glad everyone sees them— how often does anyone get to see twin great-horned owlets that close?—and the owls don't seem too disturbed at the un-invited attention.

Soon the farm is full of happy people welcoming the first vegetables of the season and revisiting their favorite Stone-bridge spots. While I'm chatting with new members, I hear squawking; some young boys have let the chickens out of the coop and I have to shoo them (the chickens, not the boys) back inside. Slippy, our irascible black goat, butts the fence next to a couple children who have been inviting her to play. "That means NO!" exclaims the little girl to her littler brother, inter-preting the body language of goats with a giggle. A returning member has brought a friend and their children for a picnic and they share the delicious "friendship bread" she baked. In the barn, Eva helps new members figure out the scales. If the weights aren't set correctly, one pound of spinach might end up filling a whole bag. "That must be too much," announces one subscriber. He's right: the pound weight was set on "one" to start rather than "zero." Weighing vegetables is a great way to teach kids mathematical skills and some common sense as well. What *does* a pound of spinach look like? Feel like? Taste like?

Opening day marks a new beginning on the farm, one that enlivens the land with the busyness of many more humans. Once the pick-up season begins on that second Saturday in May, time changes too. Each week is now marked by Satur-days, when the farm bustles with people walking and talking, slowing down their city ways, and noticing the natural world around them. Asking people to walk from the parking area below rather than drive up to the barn doesn't just increase safety on the driveway and the bridge, but creates a transitional space as they stroll up the gravel drive and cross the irrigation ditch to the barn. That walk is an invitation to enter the natural pace of the farm.

Nature does not hurry, yet everything is accomplished. From the water streaming in the ditches to the grass growing in the meadow and the birds chirping in the trees, nothing on the farm says, "Hurry." We have to slow down to match nature's pace. To live and work on the farm, we must come to a different understanding of "accomplishment," one not measured by our résumés or awards or bank accounts, but by how well we care for this land and each other, our small part in sustaining the greater world around us.

After we've picked and counted and greeted and welcomed and toured and talked, John and I walk back to the house for lunch and naps. Opening day has been perfect this year, the kind of spring day when working outside feels like play. We are grateful for the community of Stonebridge members that returns us to the fields each day. The start of another farm season has begun with its familiar rhythm: We work, we wait, and the earth gives again.

Like a sturdy and steadfast apple tree, my fifth-grade teacher inspired our first Earth Day lesson of caring for the natural world.

The First Earth Day—And Still Counting

On April 22, 1970, the first Earth Day, I was a student in Mr. Osborn's fifth grade class at Sherwood Elementary. Between the Vietnam War and the dawning awareness of environmental degradation in the late 1960s, sometimes the world seemed a pretty dark place. But in Mr. Osborn's fifth grade class, we students felt the hopefulness of a world blooming with new and exciting possibilities. Under Mr. Osborn's gifted teaching, we engaged with important social events of the times in our own youthful way.

The first Earth Day was organized by Wisconsin senator Gaylord Nelson to bring national attention to the growing problems of environmental degradation through grassroots actions focused on issues in local communities. On Earth Day, people were asked to demonstrate care for an earth whose gifts of clean air, water, and soil could no longer be taken for granted. Earth Day would not only create awareness of the steadily declining health of the environment, but bring hope of a better future for the planet.

Our fifth grade class decided to join the first Earth Day celebration by turning the hard dirt outside our classroom into a beautiful garden of grass and flowers. All it would take, we thought, were some shovels and a few seeds. On April 22, we showed up with tools—the girls wearing pants, which wasn't normally allowed—and worked like crazy all day to get that small square of soil ready for the plants we imagined would grow there. Mr. Osborn even let me run the block home for my wagon to haul away rocks and trash. With rakes and hoes in our young hands, we scratched tiny furrows in the soil to plant our hopeful seeds. A little water, a little weeding, and we'd have our first Earth Day garden. At the end of the day, we were dirty and tired, but proud to be part of something bigger than ourselves.

Around the world, twenty million participants representing thousands of schools and communities organized events like ours, from planting trees to picking up trash along highways, in what Senator Nelson called a "spontaneous response at the grassroots level." Earth Day proved that many people did care about the environment, becoming a symbol for the new ecological movement that seemed to promise cleaner air and water, healthier food, more prudent use of natural resources, and more diligent preservation of wilderness.

Thirty-six years later, I produced a digital story about our Earth Day project to commemorate that time as one seed of my environmental advocacy. After I finished the video, I decided to send it to Mr. Osborn to let him know how much he had influenced my ecological activism. I wasn't certain he was still living, but I found his name in the directory, sent off the DVD, and kept my fingers crossed.

Three weeks after I mailed my package, I was thrilled to receive a letter from my fifth grade teacher. Amazingly, he remembered me after decades of teaching hundreds of students—but that's the kind of teacher he was. Mr. Osborn made each student feel important because to him, they were. We continued to correspond and I visited him at his home, where he joked in his familiar way about retirement and getting older. He was the same teacher he had always been, enthusiastic about my pursuits and inspiring as a role model who filled his life with new interests after a long career in teaching.

Too soon after we reunited, Mr. Osborn passed away. At his memorial service, I spoke of how Mr. Osborn inspired us to engage with the important issues of our time. I said that exceptional teachers like him stand as guideposts for their students who continue to live those lessons every day. As I looked across the sanctuary full of teachers, I saw teary eyes and nods from those who had watched their own students grow. I asked everyone to commemorate Mr. Osborn's Earth Day lessons by planting a tree on the approaching fortieth anniversary of Earth Day. We planted one at Stonebridge, an Opalescent apple tree to remember Mr. O, as he was often called. At the planting, I read Rainier Maria Rilke's poem "The Apple Orchard," which speaks of an apple tree's strength to bear a heavy load of apples on its branches without breaking, "almost past endurance." The poem's last line described Mr. O's teaching as well:

Thus must it be, when willingly you strive
throughout a long and uncomplaining life
committed to one goal: to give yourself!
And silently to grow and to bear fruit.

Like a sturdy and steadfast apple tree, Mr. O committed himself to his students, the fruit that he helped nurture in a world just beginning to realize the threats to its ecological systems.

Today, Earth Day and its message of stewardship are still part of many school curriculums. Children learn about the value of recycling, saving energy, and protecting endangered species. Since the first Earth Day, the public has pushed the government and industries to enact stricter standards for air and water pollution, make cars more fuel efficient, and recover many contaminated areas. But four decades after the first Earth Day, we are living that fearful future of vanishing species, toxic food, oil spills, nuclear disasters, and climate-change-amplified weather crises.

In fifth grade, I believed that solutions to the world's environmental problems would be achieved in my lifetime. How naïve I was to underestimate the economic forces that value profit over preservation and the lack of political will to challenge them. The view that the earth is only ours for the harvesting has led us to disregard its limitations. Certainly, we should all participate in "green" efforts to plant school gardens, recycle our cans and bottles, or eat locally grown organic vegetables as ways to honor the earth as our home, yet actions like these alone will not save the planet from environmental devastation. The changes needed to stop further ecological damage are monumental—not only for the policies required but for the political will necessary to institute them—and our individual efforts so small, it's hard to see how the tiny seeds of stewardship planted so many years ago can still grow.

Like Mr. Osborn, John and I are teachers, so one of our missions at Stonebridge is to educate about the important place of organic food production in a healthy community and a healthy planet. We routinely welcome students of all ages to learn more about community supported agriculture and sustainable farming methods by working with us at the farm. We want to help students think about the future of food in both globalized and local food systems and to understand the tradeoffs between an agricultural efficiency model—with its chemical dependency, monocropping, monopoly of food and seed production, and externalizing of environmental and health costs—and an ecology model—organic pest management, crop diversity, small-scale, local control of resources, and preservation of clean water, air, and soil for the health of the planet and all its inhabitants.

While we chat and work with our hands in the soil, we ask the students to consider the costs—economic, environmental, and social—of eating oranges in Colorado in the winter and our willingness and ability to pay for them. The students think for a moment and then start listing: chemicals to grow them blemish-free in monocultured, pesticide-maintained orchards, hybridization for uniform shape and size, and fossil fuels to transport them. On the other hand: jobs provided by a citrus industry dependent on export, the health benefits of oranges, and their integration into U.S. cuisine. John and I are old enough to remember the song touting orange juice "with natural vitamin C from the Florida sunshine tree." Yet many vegetables like kale that can be grown locally in varied climates contain as much vitamin C as oranges. Where's the jingle for that? The students shake their heads at the idea of a glass of kale juice in the morning. They'll probably continue to eat oranges in the winter but with a little more thought of the tradeoffs involved.

One weekend our friend brought four students from her college sustainability class to help us weed the newly emerging spinach and carrot beds. As we worked with hoes and horis in the soft spring sun, one young man, a former student in John's calculus class, asked me what my favorite thing was at the farm.

"Besides John?" I teased him. I have so many favorites here, I had to think a bit. The most obvious answer was community, but I thought he was asking for something more prosaic than that. "The flowers," I said, "and the chickens because they're so friendly." From the student's laugh, I don't think he'd ever heard that chickens are friendly before.

After we finished weeding, we picked radishes for everyone to take home. I told the students they could eat some as they picked. "Is *this* what a radish tastes like?" one asked in wonder. "I've never tasted one like this before."

"That's because," another friend said, "you can't get a fresh radish at a grocery store. Not fresh like *this* anyway."

"Fresh is a flavor," I told them. "*This* is what fresh tastes like."

When we moved to the spinach bed, another student declined the offer of spinach. "I don't like spinach," she assured us.

"Just try a leaf, okay?" She tentatively chewed a piece—and then smiled.

"*This* is spinach? . . . Okay, I'll take some."

I wasn't sure whether to laugh or cry. How sad for eighteen-year-olds—from middle-class families who generally have access to raw vegetables in stores—not to know the taste of fresh vegetables, especially ones they've picked themselves. A salad bar may be the closest they come and that is just not the same as harvesting a carrot right out of the garden or getting fresh spinach as part of a CSA share. Food and the choices we make about it are woven into the fabric of our everyday lives, yet our decision-making is often reduced to what we "feel like" eating in a marketplace of ready-to-go food. Where food comes from and the conditions in which it is grown, harvested, prepared, marketed, and sold are of lesser concern to most people each day. The reasons for this lack of knowledge are complex and the factors to weigh in food choices overwhelming, but at least at Stonebridge, students encounter one other way to look at food, fresh from farm to table, from plant to plate, from soil to mouth.

Many years will pass before Mr. O's tree bears fruit in the old orchard at the edge of the farm, just as many years have passed since I planted my first Earth Day garden. When I tend that tree, I remember how Mr. O inspired us to care about the natural world by getting our hands in the soil. He taught us the Earth Day lesson of working together to care for our environment by visualizing the world in which we wanted to live. Even though the grass and flowers didn't survive long in the high traffic area outside our schoolroom, it didn't matter—the real seeds had been planted in us.

At Stonebridge, we celebrate Earth Day each year by planting a tree, but we know that planting trees on one day of the year is not enough to stop the ecological destruction that threatens all our lives. We must also join others in insisting that the environment not only be protected for ourselves, but for generations farther than we can count. It's not easy to celebrate Earth Day each year as news about nuclear disasters, oil spills, genetically modified crops, and contamination of land and water with oil and gas production fill our media spaces. As part of an organic farm, John and I and our members worry about agricultural losses from many different directions: land lost to development, crops lost to contamination from drift of pesticides or genetically modified organisms, and, increasingly, water lost from human-made global warming and drought.

But despite these concerns, apple trees continue to bear fruit, trees go on leafing, and the air after a rain still smells good. As farmers, consumers, and activists, we all keep going in the knowledge that the cycles of our seasons will continue and the hope that our best efforts will yield exactly what we need. Together we must create a new vision that inspires fresh seeds of environmental activism, one that looks not only at individual acts but also at collective intervention in the mounting crisis of our only earth.

On a farm, cultivated space is where humans and wilderness converge to form a fertile alliance.

The Lay of the Land

If you look at an aerial view of Stonebridge Farm, you'll see a long and narrow piece of land bounded on the south by Highway 66, the Ute Highway, named after the trail traversed through the Rocky Mountains for centuries by the Ute Indian people. You also can see the fence line marking the property on the west, a proper boundary running north and south in a straight line at 105 degrees, 13 minutes, and 57 seconds west longitude until it intersects a ditch on the northern end. The east edge of the farm is not straight but curves in and out like an hourglass as it follows the Highland irrigation ditch from north to south. The aerial view also shows the two other ditches—the Rough and Ready and the Palmerton—that flow through Stonebridge, bending sharply at the south end of the property as all three turn east to irrigate much larger farms on the Colorado plains. Although the ditches were made by early settlers needing water for farming at the end of the 1800s, they follow the natural limestone formations and creek beds of the geological terrain, resisting the straight-lined boundaries of maps and zones.

At the confluence of these waterways, things come together at Stonebridge. The aerial view shows the riparian environment provided by the ditches, foliage lining their watery course. The ditches irrigate old apple orchards and newly planted fields; shelter herons, eagles, and great horned owls in ancient cottonwoods; and provide swimming holes for farmers after a hot Saturday morning's pick. The farm is named after an actual stone bridge, one of the many bridges that cross the ditches and connect meadows to woods to barns to gardens.

When I look at our old aerial map or the view of our farm on Google Earth, the lay of the land looks quite different from how it feels to live here. On the map I can see the cluster of buildings on the southwest side of the property, old buildings that have served the farm well, some for nearly a hundred years. The house, the garage, the bunkhouse, the chicken coop, the barn, the chicken house turned guesthouse, the greenhouse, the tractor barn, and, in later editions, the Sunflower Community Room, the straw bale house, and the "bluehouse" all shelter, store, and sustain the daily agricultural activities of the farm. But this cluster of buildings only takes up a fourth of the land on the farm and only extends halfway back on the property. We live here in a different way from what a map can chart because the map doesn't show how we move or what spaces we inhabit as we live and farm here.

In our old house, the kitchen door is the gateway to the farm. From the mudroom attached to the kitchen, two doors lead outside, one on the east going over the stone bridge to the barn, and one on the west that heads past the clothesline, chicken coop, and goat pen and over the metal bridge to emerge between the barn and the greenhouse. Out these doors and over these bridges, we travel in loops throughout the day, crossing each other's paths as we go about the work of the farm. Reaching the barn or greenhouse, we have another choice to make: over the wooden bridge to the flower garden and north to the big east field, or straight out on the road past the tractor barn to the west field, over the far bridge by the herb garden, and then north to the bigger field.

Which route we take depends on many things. Do we need to grab tools from the end of the tractor barn? Check on the orchard or flower gardens? Which route is sunniest in winter? Shadiest in summer? Should we walk in the grass past the iris beds or stay on the road near the meadow? Whichever way we go, we probably come back the other, making a circuit around the farm many times a day.

Straight and round. Lines and circles. Direct and meandering. On the farm, these opposites converge. Fence lines and highways mark a boundary, but so do the ditches as they curve along the contours of the land. At Stonebridge, the crops are planted in rows for better management and productivity, but the rose garden is planted around a circle for wandering on the stone path or sitting in contemplation on the bench beside the arbor. A circle says, "Come in. Be embraced. Be enthralled." A row says, "Pay attention. Be serious. Be productive." Both lend beauty to the farm, a necessary convergence that feeds our bodies and our souls.

Once you start looking for lines and circles in nature, you see them everywhere. From space, the earth itself looks like a circle, but from earth, the horizon falls in a line between land and sky. A sunflower has a straight stalk with a round flowering head, called an *inflorescence*, at the top. The ecology symbol too is made up of both lines and curves. An oval with a line directly horizontal through its center, this symbol is a combination of the letters "E" and "O" to represent the words "Environment" and "Organism." Created by designer Ron Cobb for the first Earth Day in 1970, the ecology symbol stood for a new environmental movement that emphasized cooperation with the natural world rather than dominance over it.

The word "ecology" is taken from the Greek "oikos," meaning "home." Even in the letters forming the word, the interplay of straight and curved denotes a sense of home. Like the shape of O and S, "home" means being circled by love, but a home should also provide unbending support like the lines of I and K. A home is a combination of these things, all designed to give shelter and sustenance to those who live within it. From this sense of "oikos" comes the ecological perspective that the earth is a home to all organisms, not just humans, and must be respected and protected through sustainable practices. While an ecological view warns that all life is threatened by human activities that use resources dangerously, ecology also recognizes that human existence itself is threatened when our planetary home is contaminated or polluted by our own unsustainable practices.

Stonebridge Farm is not only our home, but home to thousands of living organisms, starting with those in the soil itself. Without these organisms, we couldn't grow vegetables here. In fact, more organisms probably live in soil than in all other ecosystems combined. Organic farming promotes the ecological care of the soil through the contribution of non-synthetic nutrients and biomass. Besides living organisms like microbes that help minerals or organic material decay, soil is home to insects and animals like earthworms that fertilize and cultivate the soil by breaking down plant material and aerating the soil they live in. Finding worms while we're planting or weeding tells us that our soil is healthy.

On the other hand, in farming, the word "dirt" usually refers to something devoid of life. While soil is alive with organisms in a food web that nourishes us through helping plants grow, dirt is considered something to be removed, scraped out by bulldozers in new housing developments or cleaned out from under your fingernails. If you're a farmer, though, you aspire to dirty fingernails. I can't seem to get mine clean until December or so.

Running throughout the soil on our farm is a complex structure of prairie rhizome grasses with roots up to ten feet deep. Of all the plants that live at Stonebridge, prairie grass is the plant that most defines Stonebridge for me, which may seem odd since it's not a crop we intentionally grow. Yet whenever we cultivate flowers, herbs, vegetables, or fruits, we uncover a vast web of fibrous grass roots as deep as we can dig. One species in particular, *Bromus Inernis*, commonly called Smooth Brome Grass, is a tall prairie grass that likes to invade my perennial beds, its slender stalk arching from the weight of seed heads bronzed in the July heat. Smooth Brome was introduced from Eurasia in the 1880s. Although I often curse the invasive nature of this non-native species, I can't help admire its persistence in inhabiting our arid region. From rhizome grass, I have learned that the true meaning of "grassroots" is found below the surface in the tenacious weaving of many into one. We may manage to clear out grass on the surface of the garden, but that interwoven root structure will survive, sending up new blades one day when we've got our backs turned.

As I'm digging roots out of the soil as deeply as I can, I think of Thoreau in *Walden* "making the earth say beans instead of grass." Thoreau got it right. No matter how much I dig, I know I'm outnumbered. Stonebridge's entire ten acres surely would return to prairie grass within a year if we stopped farming here. Sometimes that's a comforting thought, one that thumbs its nose at all things human. But if this land doesn't continue to be farmed, it could follow the development pattern along our highway corridor, becoming a subdivision or an atrocious strip mall after John and I are gone. We'll do what we can to prevent that. As farmers, John and I are committed to keeping our land in agricultural production by remaining rural, rather than annexing to the nearby city. We hope to continue growing food for our community for decades to come, but if we can't farm here, the grass reassures me that all will be well. Better to return the land to prairie than cover it with asphalt.

When I think of our work here at Stonebridge, I think of the word "cultivate," whose root word "cult" came from the Indo-European *quel* or *quol* meaning "to turn." Turning carries both the sense of turning, or cultivating, the soil, and the cycles of the seasons turning. A "culture" originally meant a piece of tilled land. The sense of the word "culture" meaning "human customs" came after the word "cultivate," as in tending the soil for crops. The concept of growing food, then, was prior to the concept of social practices, or perhaps was the first practice conceptualized as "culture." No wonder we celebrate food as one of the primary characteristics defining diverse cultures today.

The "agri" part of the word "agriculture" comes from the Latin *ager*, or field, originally meaning "*untended* land." *Agri* is related to the word "acre," which by the Norman Conquest in 1066 was defined as the area that a yoke of oxen could plough in one day, eventually becoming equivalent to 43,560 square feet in the United States, or 0.4 hectares in metric terms. Whether defining tended or untended land, *agri* is not just a measurement but also carries the sense of soil and the rural, or *agrarian*, practices that revolve around them.

These derivations are important because combined in the word "agriculture," they reveal the development of human existence through interaction with the land that has sustained our survival as a species. This vital yet vulnerable collaboration means that agriculture inhabits a mediated place in the earth's existence, a *cultivated space* somewhere between untended wilderness and urbanized civilization. On a farm, cultivated space is neither wild nor civilized, but something in between. Cultivation is where humans and wilderness converge to form a fertile alliance. Here the soil is tilled by humans with their tools and planted in an orderly fashion for the production of food. Once cultivated, the farm must depend on the elements—wind, water, and sun—to provide factors that humans cannot. In cultivation, we plant in rows as the cycles of the seasons turn and lines and circles draw themselves around us once again.

The ditches at Stonebridge, too, are cultivated spaces, despite their resemblance to wilderness. In their riparian ecosystem, they seem almost wild. Lush with grasses, cottonwoods, snakes, owls, herons, and muskrats, it's easy to forget that the ditches were dug by humans with domesticated animals and plows, cultivated in their own way for the benefit of agriculture and of people who needed food. Now even less waterborne animals use the ditches for travel. Bears, raccoons, coyotes, deer, elk, and even bobcat make their way along the paths created by water and trees.

A farm may be as close to wilderness as some people ever get, but it's not wild. Rather, a farm is a place where the natural and human worlds must live as harmoniously as we can manage, or perhaps, as we can imagine, for our imagination creates or limits our willingness for alliance. In *Plant Dreaming Deep*, May Sarton writes, "One cannot impose one's will upon a garden; something has already been imposed, the terrain itself, the landscape on which it is to be created." The same is true of a farm. We must always work with what was here first: the lay of the land and all its inhabitants.

When I complained one day about mice and rats getting into every corner of the farm and the vigilance necessitated by their constant presence, John teased, "Well, I guess you could move to the city." I don't want to do that. Instead, I'll live alongside all of the creatures here as best I can. This is their home too, and, undoubtedly, my presence is no less inconvenient to them than theirs can be to me. We have enough at Stonebridge—enough space, enough water, enough food, enough care—for all of us. From our privilege in owning this land comes the responsibility to use it wisely, not just for ourselves, but for every living thing found here. On this sphere, in these lines, we must learn to exist in plenitude together.

At Stonebridge, we gauge our weather and water by the Two Guides—Mount Meeker and Longs Peak.

Mountains to the West

"Dad, where's west?" I asked my father one evening as he read the newspaper in the living room. I was struggling with my science homework: the four directions on a compass. I knew north was at the top, but I didn't understand how an arrow pointing that way could help me determine where I was. I showed the compass to my dad, who was a surveyor and knew about finding one's bearings.

"I can see the big N on the compass," I said, "but where's north really?"

"Come on," my dad replied. "I'll show you." We went out to the backyard where the Rocky Mountains were still visible in the twilight.

"See the mountains? That's west. North is clockwise from there, then east, then south. If you can find the mountains, you'll know where you are."

I nodded. Now it made sense. Because we lived east of what is called the Front Range of the Colorado Rockies, the mountains I could see to our west were like the N on a compass: our way to orient ourselves when we didn't know which direction we were facing. All these years later, if I can imagine those mountains, I can find my way home.

I was born in North Dakota, but moved to Colorado when I was four. Each summer, driving north to visit our grandparents on their farms, we'd leave the Rockies behind; coming home, they would greet our return. Until I was an adult, the topography of my life moved from jagged to flat, mountains to prairie, and back again. I didn't question the difference: it would have been as startling to see mountains in North Dakota as to not see them in Colorado.

From afar, the mountains projected a constant distance that ordered the western edge of our world. But on weekend ascents up winding dirt roads, we witnessed their view from inside the panorama, as if the whole world were mountains with nothing beyond. When the weather was fine, we took long Sunday drives in our station wagon to mountainous spots that my dad had discovered while surveying. My mother would get up early to fry chicken for these trips, served with homemade potato salad, chocolate cake, and tinny Kool-Aid in aluminum cups.

Sometimes we would stop at an abandoned house in the woods, a rusted can of beans still waiting on the shelf. Other times we would picnic in a mountain meadow, spreading the food on the lowered rear door of the station wagon. On one trip we dug two tiny blue spruce—the state tree of Colorado—to plant in the front and back of our yard. They're still there, forty feet high, their lower limbs circling twenty feet around each trunk, overshadowing the corner property and modest brick house, as stately as if they had never left the mountainside.

When I got a little older, I went to the mountains as a Girl Scout to practice the motto "Be Prepared." We camped in the woods or stayed in rustic cabins, cooking our meals over campfires and honing our navigational skills on edifying hikes. We learned to make the mountain our friend by laying provisions for a journey and following the trail to the end. And we learned that when you're facing a mountain, one foot after another takes you to the top.

In those days, the top was as far as I went. What lay west of the mountains was never my concern. The Northwest seemed unreachable and California, too near the ocean. My family did drive to Washington State once to visit relatives near Seattle, but we traveled there from North Dakota, not from home, so that we could visit our grandparents as well. I never had the sense that "out West" had anything to do with the Pacific but rather with Idaho, since that's how my parents referred to childhood trips they'd taken to visit relatives there.

Growing up along the mountainous edge of the West, I didn't understand how living in the shadow of the Rockies determined the topography of my life until I moved to Maine the summer after my sophomore year of college. There I found no mountains and no prairie, but rather woods, lakes, and a boundless horizon of ocean extending east. I felt constantly disoriented, with no landmarks to guide me except the sun rising and setting each day. Mountains to the west had given me a sense of direction and the security of knowing where I was if I just looked up. Without them, I was lost.

Once I began to travel as an adult, I realized how instinctively we orient ourselves to the places we love. The first time I visited a friend in Manhattan, he pointed at the Empire State Building to the north and the World Trade Center to the south and told me to look for those landmarks if I got lost. Those buildings were points of navigation for people in New York City as much as the mountains were for me in the West. When the twin towers were demolished on 9/11, I sympathized certainly with the tragic loss of life and livelihood, but also with the loss of landmarks by which New Yorkers had ordinated their lives.

The first time I flew west over the Rockies, I couldn't reconcile the horizontal landscape below with the vertical view from the ground. I'm used to looking up at peaks, not down at them; stretched out below me for hundreds of miles, the mountains seemed as vast as the ocean had in Maine. Here was the fortress that had sheltered me nearly all my life—but from what? The only things to come over the mountains are storms and pine beetles that devastate our forests. Viewing the miles of true wilderness below, I understood how the mountains have kept me in as much as they keep whatever lies further west out.

I still live east of the Rockies, but closer now to the foothills than I did growing up. Our farm is only a couple of miles from the mouth of a canyon that leads into and over the mountains. Every day, when I look west, I see low hills of dark pines that form the first ridge of Colorado's Front Range. Beyond that gentle terrain, steeper peaks arise like a rocky backbone flexed above the prairie. Above all else juts Longs Peak and Mount Meeker, or *Nesotaieux*, the Two Guides, as they were called by the Arapahoe people who followed the river canyons for passage over the mountains. At 14,259 feet, Longs is the northernmost fourteener of the Rockies, with Meeker, in front, just under 14,000 feet.

Through most of my days, those peaks are on my left as I walk north to the fields and my right when I return south to the farmhouse. As farmers, we gauge our weather and our water by their visage as well. In the summer, we watch as storms gather across their summit. One August, a visitor from Oregon, where rains are gentler, noticed lightning bolts striking their stony faces. "I think it's going to rain tomorrow," she predicted.

"I think it's going to rain in twenty minutes," I laughed. "And it's heading this way!" Soon we were diving for cover as the storm lashed over our heads.

Being rooted in place means living under the conditions you find and adapting to the deficits and assets of that location. In the Front Range, we're never as hot or dry as out east on the prairie, but we often face blinding snowstorms that fall suddenly and hard, leaving feet of snow to dazzle in the next morning's sun. When a storm falls during the night, I'm awakened by the insistent scuff and flashing lights of snowplows and the muffled sound of car tires on the highway. I know I'll either have to get up early to scrape the ice off my windshield and drive cautiously into town, or re-plan my day to stay home until the roads are clear, taking a "snow day" of my own. But snow means water to irrigate our fields the next summer, so we don't begrudge the inconvenience of the storm. Each winter day, we glance at the mountains in anticipation of white peaks that promise much-needed moisture for our crops.

When I drive north from Boulder on a fall afternoon along the westernmost road before the foothills begin, the sunlight slants long shadows across the foothills until the last rays drop suddenly behind the peaks. The sunset is sudden, one moment bright, the next dim. Without an early first frost this year, the trees have kept their leaves long enough to turn a brilliant gold. Until the frost, we'll have a steady stream of weekend traffic past our farm as tourists travel to the mountains to watch the aspen turn and hear the elk bugle in Rocky Mountain National Park.

Even in the towns fifty miles east of here, the mountains are still dominant and still west. About eighty percent of Colorado's population lives along the Front Range, with county growth rates between ten and sixty percent since 2000. Citizens and public officials alike question whether such growth is supportable as jobs and resources like water decrease and problems like traffic congestion, air pollution, and competition for taxes increase. The impact of development on the mountains is foreboding. Our growth bumps up against them, not only for the extraction of resources they have historically given, but for the recreational opportunities that are important to the state's economy and to our standard of living. As the population booms and resources—and the natural environment—decline, many wonder how far the mountains can go. Yet it is our endurance, not theirs, that is truly in question.

Last week I was visiting a childhood friend at her art gallery in our little town of Lyons, a quaint gateway to the Rockies beyond. A young woman who had just moved to this area from New York asked us where she might find hiking trails nearby. We told her about Hall Ranch up the South St. Vrain Canyon just out of town and Rabbit Mountain near our farm.

"And is there another way to get to the mountains from here?" she wondered. "I drove up to Estes Park and it was really scary, especially on the way down. I'm afraid I'll go off the edge of the road and right over the cliff. Would it be better to drive up the Big Thompson Canyon through Loveland?"

My friend and I looked at each other, our childhood memories of that particular canyon flashing through our minds. "No," we shook our heads in unison. "That's scarier!" We told her about the Narrows, where the road winds through sheer rock walls. In 1976, a flashflood of over a foot of rain hurled a nineteen-foot-high wall of water down the canyon, washing away hundreds of homes and 145 lives before most people knew it was coming. We were in high school then and remembered the stories of people climbing to safety or being swept away by the river.

"Go up the St. Vrain, " we advised. "And don't worry—you'll get used to it."

But I don't think she believed us, and she may be right. It's not easy to adapt to the dangers of place, especially ones as momentous as mountains.

"Imagine being frightened of driving down the canyon," my daughter, who has grown up here, says when I tell her the story.

"Imagine being frightened of fish in the ocean," I respond, thinking about her hesitancy to snorkel in Hawai'i.

"Good point," she laughs.

To live with mountains to the west is to live a paradox: they impose their will upon us, yet strengthen us with their resolve. As constant as north on a compass, they survey our comings and goings in silent reckoning of the terrain we map at their feet. Beyond destiny or determination, they will stand for us longer than we can stand ourselves. Their guidance is immense and immutable, if only we learn to look their way.

Our barn is a former dairy barn, a spacious, gable-roofed building with high sides on the east and west where the haymows stand under the eaves.

Red, Red Barn

2011 marked not only the twentieth season of Stonebridge's CSA but the one hundredth anniversary of the farm itself. To celebrate both, we decided to paint the barn. We're not sure when it was last painted, but judging from the weathered wood, probably thirty or maybe even forty years had passed since its previous red coat. We thought it was time to give our century-old barn a new coat of good paint to help it last another hundred years, so we combined our annual pancake breakfast with a community barn-painting on a sunny morning in June.

Our barn is a former dairy barn, a spacious, gable-roofed building with high sides on the east and west where the hay-mows stand under the eaves. A century ago, hay was loaded into these lofts through high doors by pulleys under the roof's outer peaks and stored in the mows above the milking stalls that lined two sides of the barn. Hay could be forked down from the mows to the cows waiting to be milked in the stalls on either side of the barn. In the middle of the north and south lower-pitched sides, large wooden sliding doors provided entrances for the cows and wagons into the barn's center, open all the way to the roof's ridge.

Between the years of milking cows and growing vegetables, some of the barn stalls were turned into small rooms for storage or, according to rumors, bedrooms with green shag carpet and stereos for 1970s teenagers. With the creation of the CSA in 1992, the barn returned to its agricultural roots as a place for food distribution to members by combining many smaller rooms into four larger ones. But first, the huge center beam between the mows had to be replaced by jacking up the lofts because the barn had started to sag. Now the new beam should be solid enough to last another hundred years. We insulated one of the rooms with sliding doors and a cooling system to keep heat-sensitive vegetables fresh and, eventually, we finished the barn's center floor with slabs of the rosy sandstone, called redstone, quarried in our area. One of the first projects John and I undertook together was installation of three windows and long tables in the west distribution room, letting in more light and providing permanent display areas for each week's offerings. Someday, we plan to add larger windows along one wall, bringing even more light to the darker rooms at the back of the barn.

Even though I'd wanted to paint the barn for years, I had to admit that ever since I came up with the idea of an anniversary paint job, I was worried about this barn painting business. I worried that the rough wood would soak up buckets of paint. I worried about people climbing ladders and falling off the roof. I worried about finding the right color and feeding everyone while they worked. I worried we wouldn't get it done in a day, leaving us with a half-painted barn.

But when I woke up the day of the barn-painting, I decided I didn't need to worry anymore. We'd finish what we could. If we didn't get it done, we'd get to it later. Feeling a little lighter, I mixed up enough batter for three huge batches of Stonebridge oatmeal/cornmeal/whole wheat pancakes. Our members would bring toppings of all kinds to share, so I knew we'd have enough to feed a hungry crew of painters.

And then as I walked outside in the fresh morning air, I realized that I wasn't going to have to paint that barn alone. Like everything we do at Stonebridge, our members pitch in and the work soon gets done. Our farm's motto is "When the community feeds itself, the land and the people prosper" and that includes painting the old barn that holds our food.

After two decades as a CSA, Stonebridge runs like a well-

Red, Red Barn

oiled machine—most the time, anyway. We trust each other's skills and count on each other's enthusiasm and support to accomplish whatever we need to do, not only on Saturday mornings when we get the vegetables into the barn, but on any day when something needs doing. John and I make sure the supplies are handy or the prep work done—like buying the paint, power washing the barn walls, or mixing the pancakes—and then our friends take it from there.

With the table laden with toppings from yogurt to berries to granola and maple syrup, Sarah and Hunter mix gluten-free batter, and Tim flips the pancakes, as he does expertly every year at our pancake breakfasts. After everybody eats, Sandy and Rajni do the dishes. Then it's time to get to the barn.

Michelle, Eva the younger, and Eva the elder start painting the sunny south side before the day gets too hot. Lisa, Steve, and Joe (still glowing from headlining a local festival the night before with his band, Crow Radio) are joined by Jenny, Mike, Sarah, and Angus on the tall west side with brushes and buckets of Country Redwood paint. Ten-year-old Angus with a paintbrush reminds me of the lesson Tom Sawyer learned by tricking his friends into whitewashing Aunt Polly's fence for him: make the work seem like fun and everyone will want to do it. But we don't have to trick anyone into anything at Stonebridge; we're here to care for the land in return for its care of us—and if we have fun doing it, all the better.

With such a big crew, the lower part of the barn's west side is soon done. We worry that we don't have enough paint for the whole barn, but everyone votes to keep going, even though we're starting to sweat in the late morning sun. Michelle and Luca cheer us on from the tire swing. Lloyd bravely volunteers to climb up to the roof's ridge to paint the cupola, so John and Tim join him and soon it's done. The rooster weathervane on top looks like it could crow for the first time in years. Then Gretchen, Michael, Avi, and Sharonah come to help finish the shorter south side with a couple buckets of paint to spare. Eileen arrives as reinforcement and doesn't mind painting high on a ladder to tackle the lofty west side, so we haul up the ladders for Gretchen and John to join her, while Mike, Lisa, Tim, and Julie climb up to finish the east. Good thing we have a lot of ladders.

In the midst of this work-turned-party, a dear former member arrives with a beautiful engraved stone for our entryway, so Joe, Lloyd, and Mike take a break from painting to dig a deep hole to set it in place. We all stop working for a walk down the long drive to admire the new look of our entryway, but after a quick photo opportunity, we head back to finish the west side and start cleaning up the buckets and brushes.

With a few more brushstrokes under the eaves and a little touch-up work around the windows, we're done. We've painted the entire barn in a little over three hours with a half-bucket of Country Redwood to spare. As we stand in front of the barn to admire its bright red coat, we congratulate each other on another job well done. Then, hungry again and not ready to break up the celebration, we fire up the griddles for another round of pancakes with Jenny and Mike's homemade peanut butter ice cream, some cold watermelon, and a few beers.

Why did I worry about painting the barn? I should have known from years of experience on this farm that many hands make light work. This is the crew that can polish off a weedy bed in the remaining minutes after a pick— the same folks who show up when the tomatoes need harvesting before an unexpected first frost, and the same people who keep Stonebridge going year after year.

And now, the red, red barn is done, except for a little white trim we'll get to when the crops have settled down and the days are cooler once more. I doubt John or I will paint the barn again in our lifetimes and that feels good. Good to know that the hard work of the best kind of people can carry on beyond our time. This is how work used to get done on farms—from barn-raising to threshing crews to harvesting. We've lost that tradition in this country but maybe, in these times, working cooperatively will come back, not only out of necessity, but from desire for reciprocity in our relationships, with trust that we can count on each other.

Barns are a symbol of that tradition. In caring for ours, we are reminded how lucky we are to share this piece of land that sustains our families while bringing us closer together in community throughout the seasons. Closer in comfort and care for the land—that's the true meaning of the "C" in CSA.

My father, Robert Short, in front of the Smith horse barn, a symbol of my family's farming past.

Horse Barn, Milk Barn

I never saw a horse in the horse barn, but harnesses hung on the weathered walls and hay still covered the loft floor. My grandparents didn't like us climbing up there. They worried we might fall through the slots in the planks where years ago the hay was pushed down into the mangers below for the horses to eat. But sometimes we'd sneak up the steep stairway along the barn's thick, wooden wall, our feet fitting the hollows grooved into each step from years of heavy climbs. At the top of the steps, we'd peek into the dark vault of the gabled roof, smell the stale hay, and wonder what forgotten treasures lay hidden in the loft's dusty depth, abandoned when the horses were no longer needed for farming.

According to my mother, the family historian, the horse barn and other buildings had been moved to the Smith farm when my great-grandmother Flora's sister Edith—who was a Crum, as they used to say after a woman married to indicate into which family she'd been born—left her nearby homestead to go "out West" with her family. "Out West" was another colloquialism I heard growing up, usually referring to the two states most west of North Dakota—Idaho and Washington. Montana, lying geographically in the right direction, was not far enough away to constitute the "out" part.

My great-grandparents farmed with horses in the days before combustion engine tractors, so a horse barn was a valuable building, providing shelter not only for the horses, but for their feed. Hay was brought to the barn by wagons after it was cut in the fields and then hoisted by pulley to a door at the top of the barn loft, where it was stored through the winter. After tractors replaced horses, the barn stood empty, inhabited only by the farm cats that had their kittens in the soft hay. My grandmother would take us up in the loft to find the newborns before they'd even opened their eyes.

On our summer visits, one of our chores was feeding the cats in an old bowl outside the horse barn. After each meal, Grandma Smith would scrape the plates and pans for leftovers—skin, bones, crust—into a clean ice cream pail from our uncle's creamery, adding a little milk on top for the mother cat. Then we would take the scraps out to the barnyard, hoping to catch a glimpse of a cat. But they were wild, having found their way to the farm on their own or been abandoned by the side of the highway on which my grandparents lived, their city owners hoping that this farm would provide a more convenient home. My grandparents fed the lost cats and even gave them their shots if they could catch them. In return, the cats kept the farm buildings free of mice.

Across the barnyard from the horse barn stood a gambrel-roofed milk barn. My mother's parents quit milking cows before I was born, so that barn was cut down years later to make a new garage for my grandparents' car. Even though baby pictures show my mom and me in the farmyard with the milk barn towering in the background, I don't remember it as a barn.

But I do remember the milk barn at the Short farm. It didn't have a high loft like the other farm's barns but was a lower-roofed building into which the cows plodded from the pasture every evening. As children, we didn't understand how the cows knew when to come to the barn, lining up in their stalls to be milked by my grandfather. We didn't know how cows worked or how their udders would fill with milk after pasturing all day, but we could watch my grandpa squirt the milk, creamy and white, into the stainless steel buckets, keeping an eye out for a stray hoof as the cows switched their tails and waited patiently for my grandfather to finish. That cream would be separated from the milk in a round-topped machine on the back porch of the farmhouse and taken to the creamery in town once a week for pasteurization and sale. We children never drank that fresh milk because my parents were afraid we'd get sick from stray bacteria. Now some nutritionists say we're all less healthy than when we lived on farms because proximity to animals then strengthened our immune systems.

In later years, after Grandpa Short gave up raising cows, the milk barn slowly leaned inward and collapsed, as if swallowing itself. The horse barn on the Smith farm was torn down after my grandparents' death, when the land was sold to a neighbor who would farm it along with his own hundreds of acres of wheat. The milk-barn-turned-garage was left standing to house machinery, a lonely marker of my grandparents' former farmyard.

Not until I was older did I realize that barns symbolized a part of my family's farming history that was being lost on a national level. Barns once stood at the center of our farmyards and our food system, but as this country has turned away from its rural roots, barns have become an endangered species. Once, families depended on them to house the animals and store the food required for survival, but as agriculture became first mechanized and then industrialized, barns like those on my grandparents' farms no longer held the necessities of living on the land.

In *Grace*, photographer Gregory Spaid poignantly captures the architecture of rural America with its once noble buildings, faded but not forgotten in small towns whose livelihood still comes from the land. On facing pages in black and white tones, Spaid juxtaposes a grain elevator and a church, the two tallest structures in rural communities, signifying two different kinds of farming faith. In stark images, whitewashed barns loom ghostly as ancestors, rising from the dark prairie, determined to preserve a way of life. I remember these barns and small towns from my childhood trips to North Dakota, when weathered buildings broke the monotony of the highway and the flat land it crossed.

Our own barn at Stonebridge is a part of that rural history, but it's not the same as those old barns were to me. Our barn was saved because it continued to fit the needs of small-scale farmers on a farm that was maintained by our forward-thinking predecessors. It's the heart of the farm, a lively place where our members come each Saturday to find their weekly share. By painting our barn, we too hope to preserve it for generations to come.

We're lucky to have our original barn, but it lacks the mystery of my childhood barns. Those barns were imposing, larger than the life that had been lived in them; even when I was a child, that life was fading away. Built for a kind of farming that died out with my grandparents' generation, the horse barn and the milk barns could not outlive their use. Nor could I imagine that one day, like the farms themselves, they would be lost and my childhood summers left behind. Without those barns, the farms could no longer exist, disappearing entirely from the landscape they embellished. So I conjure them here in words that can only tell my part of their story. Preserved in memory and old photographs, those barns stand still against the prairie as hay turns to dust, boards sink, nails loosen their hold, and rusty chains drop, coiled, to the floor.

At our annual Stonebridge pancake breakfasts, members share a communal table of homemade and fresh-picked toppings.

Toppings to Share

Orange butter, apple butter, sliced apples, spiced apples, dried apples. Apple sauce, rhubarb-apple sauce, rhubarb-honey sauce. Blueberry syrup, grape syrup and, of course, maple syrup. Home-canned peaches, blueberries, vanilla yogurt, peanut butter, the biggest bowl of strawberries ever picked at Stonebridge Farm, and popcorn.

Popcorn?

Yup, popcorn.

These were the toppings at our recent pancake breakfast, an annual event held on a June Saturday right after the pick. Once all the week's vegetables are in the barn, the crew comes in from the fields to join the members for some hearty Stonebridge pancakes and a communal table of toppings, homemade and fresh-picked, shared with laughter on a beautiful summer day.

When I was growing up, I loved the folktale *Stone Soup*, in which a village hides their meat and vegetables from hungry soldiers. When the clever soldiers claim they can make a tasty soup from rocks and boiling water, the villagers offer their hidden ingredients to flavor the broth until the pot is full of enough delicious soup to feed the entire town. "I've got a few onions!" "I can find some carrots!" "How about potatoes?" the villagers exclaim, tricked by the soldiers into contributing the foods they had hidden. You can make something from almost nothing, I learned as a child, if everyone shares what they can.

At Stonebridge, our pancake breakfasts remind me of *Stone Soup*, except that everyone is happy to supply their part. I mix the pancake batter and the members graciously contribute the *real* ingredients, the ones that make standing in line for pancakes worth the wait. Deborah, whom we call our "e-barn boss" since she manages our email recipe list, says that with our recipe, "you, too, can feed scores of folks." On the Thursday before this year's pancake breakfast, I pull out our pancake recipe to make a grocery list. "Three cups of ground oatmeal. That's not much," I think, and then I remember that I need to *triple* the recipe for this occasion. Nine cups of ground oatmeal, sixteen cups of flour, three times more of everything on the ingredients list. I go to the natural foods grocery store and place a box in the bottom of the largest cart, rather than the smaller size I usually use. Then I stock up on big bags of grains and baking supplies, bottles of oil, and cartons of rice milk. When I get to the checkout, I tell the clerk we're making pancakes for a crowd and she nods. That's a lot of ingredients.

On Friday, I grind many batches of oatmeal flakes in the food processor and get out our three largest bowls, the ones I usually use for baking bread or serving a crowd-sized pasta salad. I take the three electric griddles out of their boxes, set up two tables with extension cords on the screened porch of the Sunflower Community Room, and position a griddle, spatula, and ladle next to each. Another griddle goes on the Sunflower's kitchen island for wheat-free, vegan pancakes; one of our members has volunteered to bring the batter as her "topping." I pick just-bloomed iris from the flower garden for a vase on the toppings table and set out stacks of plates and coffee cans of silverware. Everything's ready to go for tomorrow when we mix up the batter and start flipping.

We weren't always so organized for our pancake breakfasts. By the time I came to Stonebridge, pancakes were a tradition but not a routine. The pancake breakfast began as what was called a "hoe-down," when members volunteered in the gardens and were rewarded afterward with pancakes and a little bluegrass music from a local trio. Once our bartering crew was established, we no longer needed unskilled "farmers" wielding hoes in the fields, so we dropped the "hoe-down" but kept the pancakes.

In the early days, the pancake breakfast was pretty chaotic. One year, we tried to make cakes on camp stoves outside until a stove melted right through the plastic picnic table on which it sat. The next year, we put the cast-iron griddles on the stove in the kitchen, but that year the batter was extra thick and the cakes cooked too slowly, so the line wound around the house while everyone waited for their half-raw pancakes.

After that year, we bought a couple of electric griddles and ran extension cords out to the field by the tractor barn. The griddles were wonderful but the fuses kept blowing, so someone would run to the fuse box in the barn to throw the switch. Now we have the Sunflower Community Room, a renovated hog barn, for our farm events. We've rewired, added a fuse box and another electrical circuit, and moved the griddles to separate currents, but the system still needs some tinkering. At this year's event, we had to alternate flipping pancakes with running the water to wash the tons of sticky dishes because we couldn't operate the water pump and a griddle on the counter at the same time. Whatever we try, it seems blowing fuses is just a part of the Stonebridge pancake breakfast tradition.

For this year's pancake breakfast, the weather's sunny and just warm enough for T-shirts. While Tim and Paul, our veteran pancake flippers, take turns at the griddles, members wander in and out of the Sunflower Room and kids play on the giant swing over the ditch. As people come and go, the toppings are replenished and everyone gets to try something new. I'm running the whole time, trying to catch up with members while refilling batter bowls and picking up dishes. When the crowd thins out a couple hours later, I sit down with a plate of pancakes to chat with lingering friends. Some of us have been outside since 7 a.m. so it's nice to rest while we finish off the batter and whatever yummy toppings remain.

Since Stonebridge is a "share the harvest farm" in which the weekly distribution is based on the bounty of the field rather than the market value of the vegetables, our members share exactly what's ready to harvest that week. By August, when the high-summer vegetables like tomatoes, peppers, squash, and eggplant are booming, members will need many bags to carry it all home. They also experience the diversity and seasonality of foods that grow in this region, from vegetables to fruit to herbs, and can expect something new each time they come to the barn to pick up their share.

This idea of sharing extends to our pancake breakfast as well. "Toppings to share" is a concept John and I think a lot about at Stonebridge. To us, it means encouraging relationships in ways that build community. The phrase itself comes from our pancake breakfasts: when we send around an email to the members or write an announcement for the event on our barn chalkboard, we always include the phrase "toppings to share." That's because in one of our earliest years, we failed to specify that people should bring pancake toppings to eat communally. Instead, we wrote something like "bring whatever toppings you'd eat at home." People interpreted that to mean "only bring enough toppings for yourself," so they brought half a banana, a tiny container of yogurt, or the almost empty jar of peanut butter from their cupboard. What a terrible pancake breakfast *that* was.

We learned at that breakfast that if we mean "to share," we need to say it. If the meal is communal and will benefit from everyone's participation, it's up to us to make that intention perfectly clear. At the very next farm meal event—the annual Halloween party on the last Saturday of the season—we spelled it out: bring finger foods *to share*. And everyone did.

In this country's rural history, agricultural communities were dependent on sharing and cooperation. Events like barn raisings and grain threshing were communal events where neighbors helped each other. They borrowed each other's tools, horses, and machinery; they met for quilting bees, butchering, and food preserving. After the work was done, someone brought out a fiddle and they danced and sang together. The *Little House* books by Laura Ingalls Wilder on which I was raised have delighted generations of readers with heartwarming stories of a time when the fate of families and neighbors were joined by their common need for food, shelter, and companionship.

In the highly individualized consumer culture of the US today, sharing is a custom we rarely practice. Sharing is inconvenient—we want things when we want them, not later. John says that moving is the last vestige of cooperation in our culture. We help each other pack, lift, load, haul, unload, and unpack again, but after the work of moving is done, we're on our own. As consumers, we're supposed to purchase all the tools, technology, and goods we need for ourselves, rather than own them communally. We buy what we need rather than borrow it. That way, we don't have to be responsible for returning it. On the other hand, we hesitate to lend things because we are afraid we won't get them back. It's the *ethics* of sharing we've lost as much as the practice, an ethics that says we can cooperate on fulfilling our needs if we respect that one person's need is as important as the other's.

Traveling in both the countryside and the urban areas of Cuba, John and I learned important lessons about sharing. In Cuba, if you only have a cup of beans, that's what you share. Guests are offered the best of what there is, even if the host goes with little. There, hospitality is about gracious giving rather than material objects. In Cuba, we saw this gracious hospitality offered over and over again without hesitation or worry; even when there's just a little bit of something to offer guests, it's given in the spirit of generosity. Once, when our dinner plans fell through because the *paladar*, a restaurant in a private home, we had intended to dine at was closed, the neighbors volunteered to make us a dinner of chicken, rice and beans, salad with cucumbers and tomatoes, bread, and fried plantains. Of course, we paid them for their food and labor, but I don't think we could have compensated them for their time or for the friendly and warm conversation we enjoyed while the simple but delicious food was prepared. The oldest son was a chef who even shared the secret of Cuban Black Beans with us: oregano and cumin, plus a *sofrito* of sautéed onions, green peppers, and garlic. That's how I make them today, and they taste like Cuba to me.

Our members give back the produce the land has offered by joining it with their culinary creativity at Stonebridge potlucks. We find joy at this sharing, whether it's roasted vegetables with flavorful herbs, homemade bread warm from the oven, or something as simple as chopping mint on a raspberry and melon salad. Lots of people have their special potluck recipe. Gretchen always brings her delicious polenta dish topped with a medley of that particular week's vegetables. Deirdre bakes her sumptuous shortbread, the kind that melts in your mouth. Renee and Dave bring wonderfully flavored beans, in addition to whatever innovative dish they've prepared from Stonebridge's weekly share. I'm especially enamored of the homemade cheese crafted by Lyn and Drew with milk from their goats. Great food doesn't require hours in the kitchen, just some creativity and attention. The best food, to me, tastes of the fresh ingredients that went into the dish, prepared with care, and shared with love.

Over the years, when we've invited younger people to potlucks, they've asked, "What should I bring?" We explain it's not only *what* they should bring but also *how much* that counts. When you come to a potluck, you want to feed as many people as possible. If someone doesn't know how to cook yet, we tell them to bring chips and salsa or bread from a local bakery. When one of our young bartering members discovered *The Joy of Cooking*, it opened a whole new potluck world for him.

"If only I'd known," he exclaimed. It hadn't occurred to me that he didn't know about cookbooks. Now when someone young asks what to bring, I mention it.

When I was in college, my women's book group had a potluck for our discussion of the newly published novel *The Women's Room* by Marilyn French. My good friend Teresa had made five-bean salad with kidney, cannelloni, pinto, garbanzo, and green string beans with an oil and vinaigrette dressing. The only problem was, she'd strapped the salad bowl to the back of her bike. By the time she got to the potluck, all of it had bounced out except exactly five beans. We were sorry to miss the salad but appreciated her intention and the labor behind it. I don't remember what anyone else made for that dinner, but I'll always remember Teresa's five-bean salad for the feminist sisterhood it embodied.

I know that we're spoiled at Stonebridge, that not everyone takes potlucking as seriously as we do. A friend and former bartering member who moved far away to a suburban neighborhood back east lamented the loss of Stonebridge potlucks. A potluck there, she found, meant deli take-outs in tiny containers along with lots of hot dogs. What's wonderful about Stonebridge potlucks is the irresistible variety of foods shared, all at one meal. I love to take a little bit of everything in a sampler plate. Potlucks are *beautiful* too, the way homemade bread lies crustily on the handmade maple chopping block, hearty beans and vegetables bubble in earthenware casserole dishes, and the vibrant green, red, and yellow of butterhead lettuce and heirloom tomatoes blushing in a vintage salad bowl.

Meals like these are the community's way to feed each other with a little special effort, sharing some of the best of what we each have to offer. I always leave a Stonebridge gathering feeling not only full of food, but also full of new ideas for preparing the vegetables we've grown. Each dish is an unexpected gift that extends the knowledge and talents of our community, and each meal, the collaboration of sweet and savory dishes from many different family histories and cuisines. Like the fabled stone soup, Stonebridge potlucks create a feast much richer than what any of us could make on our own. With a little of this and a little of that, the sum is far greater than the parts because the food is shared with laughter and gratitude for how each has gone *a little further* to feed us all that day.

Going a little further is a lesson seen in the natural world as well. Nature is not stingy with its gifts but offers them when the conditions are right. Vita Sackville-West, best known as Virginia Woolf's companion and a journalist in her own right, wrote of Nature's prodigiousness in her gardening column for the *Observer*, "I like generosity wherever I find it, whether in gardens or elsewhere." Henry Beston echoes this sentiment in *The Outermost House*, his 1928 chronicle of a solitary year on Cape Cod. Watching small fish attempt an inland migration from sea to brook, he "began to reflect on Nature's eagerness to sow life everywhere, to fill the planet with it, to crowd with it the earth, the air, and the seas."

Beston was contemplating ocean life, but his words are true of seeds as well: sowing seeds everywhere is one of the things Nature does best. Nature is an indiscriminate giver, asking not to whom its gifts are given but only for the chance to be received. The delivery may be random, but what lavishness comes of this offering should inspire us all. This is the harder lesson to learn from Nature's graciousness: to give without expecting in return, to let the giving be enough.

If the pancake breakfast and our solstice anniversary mark the start of summer, John's birthday in mid-August and the local Folksfest concert mark its end. Soon the farm children will head back to school and we'll all start to contemplate cooler weather. The zucchini, however, don't know that our summer is almost over—they're just ramping up for another month of heavy picking. I secretly make John a carob zucchini cake for his birthday and sneak it out to the field on Saturday morning to share with the barterers who are picking French *haricot verts*, the plants hanging so full of skinny beans that each picker can squat in the same place for quite a while before moving down the row. Before John notices the cake, Julie sticks a bean in each piece as a "beandle" instead of a candle, and then we all sing happy birthday as John pretends to blow the beandles out in one big breath. But he's missed a few and has to take an even bigger breath to extinguish them fully. The cake is so moist with squash, we don't need plates or forks as we joke about birthdays in the bean patch.

Now come the days of heavy harvest, the weeks when members look in consternation at the long list on the barn board and we apologize to everyone for the many bags they have to carry from the barn. "I didn't quite eat everything I got last week," they apologize back.

"That's okay," I reassure them. "The garden won't mind."

Our members have always appreciated nature's bounty. They know that a "share the harvest" farm also means that we get what we get. If the zucchini fail, which has unimaginably happened, no one gets zucchini. If hail ruins our crops—which has yet to happen--the shares may be minimal that season. We offer no promise, no guarantee, no money back. Lucky for us, we may have had less than conducive conditions or a crop failure for certain vegetables, but we've never had to shut down the barn. Our members trust us to do the best we can and they're always happy to help, whether the problem be too much or too little. Members in the truest sense of belonging, they offer encouragement for our efforts in the fields, like the poem of magnet words I found on our barn fridge:

Yes
Go Farmer
Please Homegrown
Many Better Legendary Harvest Be Always
We Need Organic Love Good Hope

A Bushel's Worth

When seeds scatter in the wind, they go a little further afield. When humans practice generosity, they go a little further too. The best sharing is when we give like nature does, freely and without expectation of return. We forget, sometimes, this ethic of sharing that lets the seeds fall where they will. Like "toppings to share," we all need a reminder from time to time that when we bring the best we have to the table, our sharing is the real reward.

Stonebridge Pancakes

3 cups rolled oats ground lightly in a food processor until chopped but not floury (about 4 1/2 cups pre-ground)
6 cups whole-wheat pastry flour
3 cups cornmeal (not polenta)
6 Tbl baking powder
3 tsp salt
6 eggs
6 Tbl maple syrup
1/4 cup safflower, sunflower, or vegetable oil, plus some for the griddle
8-9 cups rice milk

In a large bowl, mix the dry ingredients. This can be done a day ahead and refrigerated until needed.

In a separate bowl, whisk the eggs and add the maple syrup and oil. Add this mixture to the dry mixture and blend. Stir in 8 cups of rice milk until blended, adding more rice milk until reaching the desired consistency. The batter should pour easily from a ladle onto the pre-heated, lightly oiled 380° griddle to form a circle without running. Pour about 1/4 cup of batter onto the pre-heated griddle, forming a 4-inch cake. When small bubbles appear on the top of the cake, flip it and cook until the cake can easily be lifted from the griddle.

Triple this batch to serve 100 people or so with toppings to share.

The wheat silos stand sentry at the edge of the Short farmyard.

Silos

Bedtime is approaching at our grandparents' farmhouse. The northern twilight has lingered as long as it can; now darkness spreads across the prairie, made even blacker by the absence of the moon.

My little brother and youngest sister have already brushed their teeth with well water splashed into a basin from the long-handled pump in the kitchen. (I will be a teenager before city water will be piped to the farmhouse and we can brush our teeth with water from a faucet.) Now in their pajamas, the two are tucked into the hide-a-bed in the living room, ready for the night.

But something is missing: my brother's stuffed bear, Gentle Ben. We search the house, but the bear isn't there. He must be outside.

"Kayann, can you find Gentle Ben? You know where you were playing." My mother hands me a flashlight. I am nine or ten, the oldest of four children, and it's my job to take care of my brother and sisters. We are visiting my Grandma and Grandpa Short's North Dakota farm, and my four-year-old brother's stuffed bear is lost somewhere in the tall grass where we had been playing. Without Gentle Ben, my brother will not go to bed. He cries as I take the flashlight in my hand and open the screen door off the kitchen porch where my grandfather processes the milk from his few dairy cows each day.

That afternoon, my two sisters and brother and I had been down in the tall grass by the narrow dirt road that crossed the countryside in front of my grandparents' farm. Years later, the road was paved to create a highway between the Canadian border and the county seat twenty-five miles from the farm, but in my childhood it remained a rural road, travelled mostly by farm families heading back from the city or by tractors coming in from the fields. In the summer, we could spot a car in the distance by the dust it raised before we could see the car itself.

The roadside seems an odd place to play, but the grass is highest where the spring rains run off the road into a ditch along the edge. The ditch is dry now but the moisture has done its work: the grass is taller than my littlest sister's head. On hot summer afternoons until dinner, we play hide-and-seek by tromping the grass into shelters under which we can burrow. Gentle Ben must be there now, hiding alone in the dark.

Flashlight in hand, I step out into the darkness. Sunset comes late on the North Dakota prairie, so as kids we often go to bed before the sky is truly dark or the stars have emerged. But this night the search for Gentle Ben has delayed our bedtime and the sun has already fallen behind the long horizon.

I don't know how far the farmhouse is set back from the road, but it surely seems longer than a city block at home. I walk from the kitchen door to the end of the stone path that meets the edge of the driveway stretching down to the road. Silent barns stand across from the house, the chickens and cows long since sleeping.

I've never been outside alone before, at least not like this. The night is blacker in the country, where no lights can be seen. Within the glare of street lamps or the glow of a neighbor's porch light slanting across a lawn, cities are never really dark, but nighttime in the country is complete.

Shining the flashlight across the gravel, I start toward the road and the grass where we played. In the dark, I can't see where I'm headed, but I know which direction to walk. I swing the flashlight's beam to the left across my grandmother's flower garden and then right against the wheat silos standing sentry at the farmyard's end. Acres of pasture lie beyond those silos. Wandering there, I could truly be lost, so I turn the flashlight back to the driveway and keep walking.

I don't remember ever being afraid of the dark, even though I sleep alone in a basement bedroom at home, but inside dark and outside dark are not the same. Until tonight, I have never seen the sky so black nor so filled with stars. How could a universe so large consider the smallness of me worth protecting as I walk slowly toward grasses still lost from my view?

But I'm not afraid. I'm exhilarated to be alone in the world, without sisters or brothers to care for, without parents to tell me what to do. Darkness, I realize, is just a cover for sunlight. Everything at night stays exactly the same as it is in the day; you just can't see it as clearly.

When I grow up and live at Stonebridge Farm, I'll get a call in the middle of the night from the police asking me to check the license plate on my car. Another car with the same number has been involved in a hit-and-run accident. After verifying that it is indeed the police on the phone, I will fumble outside without caution or contact lenses, find my license plate intact, phone the police with the good news, and go back to bed. In the morning, John will show me the bear prints near the back door. Maybe if I wear glasses next time I make a midnight ramble, I will notice them.

But on my grandparents' farm, another bear is waiting. As I edge down the gravel driveway toward the long grass that hides Gentle Ben, I turn off the flashlight and let the night sky conceal me in blackness. I don't think of words like "shroud" or "cloak" for the dark, and I'm not afraid. I look back to see the light of the farmhouse shining through the curtains. Everyone else is inside that light. I am outside, as alone as I'll ever be.

We stood the sheaves on end, balanced bundle to bundle in a circle to form a shock.

A Bushel's Worth

"Do you think we could grow wheat here?" Paul, our bartering friend, asked one fall. We thought about it for a minute and then agreed it wouldn't hurt to try. One little field wouldn't necessarily feed us, but if we could grow our own wheat, we'd be that much closer to self-sufficiency. We already grew our own vegetables and logged our own wood for heat. If we grew wheat, we could buy a flour grinder and mill our own grain. From that, we could make our own bread and pasta. Never mind that flour in bulk is relatively inexpensive or that baking bread takes time we rarely seem to have. First, we would see if we could even grow wheat. How much work could it be?

The next September, John planted an 8 x 75-foot bed of red winter wheat in the east field, in view of the foothills. The seed emerged from the ground just before its winter dormancy, strengthening the wheat and giving it a head start on spring growth. After a winter's rest, the wheat grew beautifully through the cool spring, the stalks tall and straight and the heads fattening and finally ripening in the hot summer sun.

I loved watching the wheat grow. It reminded me of my grandparents' fields, the wheat swaying in the hot North Dakota wind under the sheer blue sky when we visited each summer. My grandfathers used to pick a head or two to test for ripeness and moisture. They knew exactly when to harvest because knowing meant getting the best price. Once the harvested wheat was stored in huge, round metal bins, my father would trickle a little out through the spigot for us to chew like bubble gum. Ripening in the summer field, our Stonebridge wheat seemed like a descendent of those kernels.

The third week of July, with the temperature pushing 100°, the wheat was ready for harvest. A crew of bartering members came out on Thursday morning to help with the momentous task. John cut neat swathes of grain with the sickle bar mower on the tractor, the wheat falling in perfect rows along the ground. Now what to do? We decided to bundle the wheat into sheaves an armful wide to make loading the wagon easier. Working along the rows, we each picked up as much as we could carry and laid the bundle on top of a long strand of baling twine stretched out on the nearby grass by one of the crew. Tying the twine around each sheaf, we threw it up onto the hay wagon as high as we could toss.

Working in the hot sun with sweat running down our faces, we gathered the wheat carefully with the seed heads bunched at one end of a compact bundle so that the sheaves wouldn't fall apart. Some of us wore conical straw hats like those of Asian rice farmers and others wished for long sleeves to protect their arms from the scratching stalks. Bending, gathering, bunching, and tying, we moved slowly down the fallen rows of sun-warmed wheat. Arms wide, we literally embraced the harvest. After several hours in the withering sun, the field was clean and the wagon was stacked with fat sheaves of golden wheat.

Before the wheat kernels could be separated from the stalks, the sheaves needed to dry. We laid tarps on the ground between the tractor barn and the Sunflower Room on which to stand the gathered sheaves. Working together, we stood them on end, balanced bundle to bundle in a circle to form a shock. The sheaves had to be placed as upright as possible so they would lean against each other and not tip over from their own weight. If the center sheaves didn't hold, the outer sheaves wouldn't provide a strong enough support to keep standing. Soon we had enough sheaves to form three broad shocks. Against the weathered wood of the tractor barn, they summoned a by-gone era when their thick kernelled plumage promised loaves of hearty bread for a winter's sustenance.

Harvesting the wheat from the field is only half the work. A week after our harvest, another crew came to thresh the wheat by separating the kernels from the stalks. With such a small amount to thresh, we would do it by hand, but we weren't quite sure how. The earliest recorded method involved hitting the wheat on the ground with flails. We didn't have any medieval flails, so we moved on to a later historical mode. The original meaning of "thresh" is to tread or trample grain with horses or oxen on a threshing floor. Having no large animals, we made do by laying the sheaves on a tarp and, with our stocking feet, rolling the seed heads against the ground to separate them from the stalk, an efficient but wearisome method.

A few of our world-traveling members had seen threshing in other countries accomplished by whacking the sheaves against a wall or a log, so next we improvised with a picnic bench placed on a tarp. As we whacked, we joked that we were using more calories threshing the wheat than we would gain from eating it. Maybe "thrashing" would be a more accurate term, a word derived from "threshing" and often used in place of it, although more commonly meaning hitting or striking, as in "give them a good thrashing." My mother says "threshers" more like "thrashers," a regional pronunciation that I've adopted in deference to my North Dakota roots.

As the kernels separated from the stalks, the husks and chaff needed to be removed. In earlier times, this winnowing was simply accomplished by throwing the grain into the air or tossing it up and down on a cloth, but one barterer remembered watching Indian farmers use a fan to blow off the chaff while they threshed, so we ran an extension cord out to the harvest site. The fan did blow the broken bits of stalk and chaff away from the heavy kernels, but most of it ended up back on the tarp anyway. At least the fan helped cool us as we worked.

Since the kernels on the tarp still held a lot of debris from the broken stems and outer husks, we needed to clean them before our harvest work was done. Here's where mechanization could come in. We own a seed-cleaning machine that shakes the seeds from top to bottom through progressively finer screens, until the seeds roll off the bottom screen into a bucket. After picking out the largest debris by hand, we poured the kernels through the seed machine in several batches and finished with clean grain.

How much wheat did we produce from one long bed and two mornings' harvest work? Seventy pounds of wheat kernels: about a bushel's worth. Enough to grind a little into flour, use some for sprouting, and add a little chewiness and fiber to John's daily oatmeal, but not much for a dozen people's labor, not to mention John's plowing, planting, and mowing. Now I fully appreciated the hard work of my grandparents and great-grandparents on their North Dakota prairie farms. I grew up hearing about wheat harvests and cooking for threshers, but I never realized that the machinery called a *com*-bine was named so because it com-*bined* the jobs of mowing the crop, threshing the wheat heads from the stalk, and separating the wheat kernels from the chaff with just one huge machine, leaving the leftover straw in the field for baling.

For my mother growing up on a North Dakota farm, much depended on the wheat. She remembers my grandmother whispering, "Wait until we sell the wheat," when my mom would ask for new shoes, whispering because parents didn't discuss money with children in those days. The wheat harvest's success meant the difference between a prosperous or a lean year, with most of the factors behind its success—sun, rain, and the markets that determined the price—out of a farmer's hands.

In Meridel LeSueur's 1929 short story "Harvest," a young, newly married couple, farming immigrants to the United States, quarrel over whether to buy a threshing machine for wheat. The husband, with his "new world cunning to know," believes that the machine represents progress and will secure them an important place in the community. Ruth, the wife, dreaded the machine, viewing it as "an encroachment like another woman or war" on their marriage. Her husband doesn't understand her fear, complaining to the other men that she "wants to keep the old way, God knows why." Ruth is certain the change from harvesting by hand and horse to threshing with the "cold, mindless" machine will threaten their happiness: "She couldn't say why she was so afraid but she knew it was against her and against him. It was a new way."

The old way, for Ruth, is tied not only to the Old Country but also to the earth itself with its "ancient closed fertile life." LeSueur connects the old ways of farming to the couple's sexual relationship, for Ruth is pregnant with their first child, something she hides from her husband in her anger about the machine. Once he finds out, he uses the baby to argue for the purchase of the machine: "We've got to get ahead, you know that. Now more than ever, haven't we?" Yet when he buys the thresher, he too fears "leaving the moistness of sleep, the old world of close dreaming in the thick blossomed surface" they have shared.

In this story, LeSueur captures an important transition in early twentieth-century agriculture as mechanization began to make farming more dependent on capital than on labor. Farmers who could afford the new machines—in this story, bought with the wife's dowry—could get ahead of their neighbors by threshing crops more quickly and with fewer laborers, perhaps even renting the equipment to others. While a century later, such modernization may seem unquestioningly beneficial, even essential, to farming, LeSueur's story cautions that something ineffable will be lost as machines replace human hands in the soil—"the space of mystery where the seed unfolds to the touch in the cool and thick and heavy sap, the world of close dreaming that is like a woman's hair or the breasts of men."

Readers may understand the husband's desire for progress, but LeSueur clearly meant for us to sympathize with Ruth and her attachment to "the old ways." By marking the transition from human labor to machine, LeSueur's story predicts the destruction of family farms that will change the face of farming over the rest of the twentieth century. Looking back, we can trace such mechanization as one factor in the rise of larger and eventually corporate-owned industrial farms that left small-scale family farms behind. As the local agriculture movement challenges the industrial farming model, the question of mechanization should be revisited, even as technological advances change farming again. What is the role for human labor and what for machines in farming today?

After our Great Wheat Harvest, we all agreed that wheat was better grown with some mechanization and in larger acreage than we had attempted, much as my grandparents had done. But growing, harvesting, and threshing our own wheat, as small a yield as it was, also taught us the sheer physical labor that our ancestors' subsistence farming required. Although we're still skeptical about the sustainability of corporate-run, industrial-scale farming, we can see both the benefit of farms larger than ours growing organic wheat and the necessity for smaller-scale machinery that fits farms like ours as we all rethink a bushel's worth, big and small.

My mother, Karen Smith, between her older sisters Lola and Del Vera with their Victory Garden vegetables.

Cooking for Threshers

In a gabled farmhouse, overalled men sit at a long, checker-clothed table in the dining room, while the women cook over a woodstove in the kitchen and serve the men from large platters of food. The 1934 painting *Dinner for Threshers* by the regionalist painter Grant Wood, best known for his painting of the stoical rural couple in *American Gothic,* illustrates how the women in the family worked just as hard inside getting meals on the table during those busy harvest days as the men did working outside.

My mother, Karen Kay Smith Short, grew up cooking for threshers along with her mother, Geneva Walker Smith, her grandmother Flora Hunsley Smith, and her older sisters Del Vera and Lola. I have a black and white photograph of the three sisters as young girls sitting on the steps of their farmhouse holding baskets of vegetables that have just been picked from their farm garden. I call it "The Victory Garden" after the World War II national call for home gardening because the photo was taken around that time, but my grandparents always grew their own vegetables, not just as part of the war effort.

My mother's memories of cooking for threshers portray not only the incredible *quantity* of food cooked, but also the pride the women took in the *quality.* When my mother was growing up in the 1930s and 40s, her Grandma Flora cooked for the neighborhood threshing crew that came to the Smith farm each August when the wheat was ready to harvest. My mother remembers the dining room table set and waiting for the men with homemade butter, pickles, relishes, jams, and jellies and plates of fresh bread at each end. Once the hungry threshers arrived from the fields, the women passed around heaping platters of food raised or grown on the farm. The menu varied daily from roast beef and onions, fried chicken, ham, Swiss steak with tomatoes, chicken-fried steak with cream gravy, creamed chicken on baking powder biscuits, or my great-grandmother's specialty—pork ribs with sauerkraut and apples—along with fresh or home-canned vegetables, often creamed because my great-grandparents milked their own cows.

At least two kinds of pies or cobblers finished the meal before the men went back out to the fields. Only then did the women sit down to eat, taking a short rest before they washed the piles of dishes and began preparing sandwiches, cakes, and cookies for the men's mid-afternoon snack. But the day didn't end until they'd cooked another big meal to serve after the sun had set and the men came in to eat. Then the men would go home to do their own chores, while the women started baking bread and desserts for the next day's threshing meals.

According to my mother, "The threshers bragged about women who were good cooks in the neighborhood and my Grandma Flora was one of them. But for all of us just learning to cook, 'cooking for threshers' probably had an emotional tie that shaped our thoughts about cooking *enough*. To watch those farm men and boys eating hungrily and heartily, we, the new cooks in the family, worried about whether we had prepared enough food for the meal. We sure didn't want to be the family in the neighborhood whose food had run out before the men were full!" My mother's last line says it all. A woman's reputation, and hence her family's, rested on her ability to provide enough food, and of delicious quality, for the threshing crews.

My mother grew up cooking for threshers, but once she married my father, who had become a surveyor rather than take over the family farm, she continued to help my grand-mother as long as we lived in North Dakota. When I was just over a year old, my grandmother's back was bothering her so much that she had to stay in bed and my mother had to cook by herself for the threshing crew. By that time, my grandfather had a modern combine that made the work easier, so the crew was smaller, but they were still hungry. My mother remembers my grandfather assuring her that she could do it, so my grand-mother took care of me while my mother cooked for several days. In fact, my grandmother, a former schoolteacher, taught me the word "NO" while we played and read books in her bed-room, something my mother did not appreciate at the time and probably still doesn't.

When my sisters and I get together for family meals, we joke about "cooking for threshers." To my youngest sister Kar-lene, "cooking for threshers" means "cooking a lot of food for a lot of people (men mostly I guess)." The gendered notion of hungry farm men persists for my mother: she once jumped up from the table to exclaim, "John, your plate is empty!" as if someone had stolen his food.

To my sister Kari, who is two years younger than I am and was also born in North Dakota, "cooking for threshers" sum-mons memories of our Grandma Smith: "I could really go for some of her cinnamon and sugar donuts, cinnamon rolls, homemade bread and her delicious lemon meringue pie, still my favorites. Mom always said they had to fix a lot of food for the threshing crew. I think poor Grandma had to spend her whole day cooking, driving out to the fields, then cleaning up after each meal. I don't know how she did it."

Kari's right that Grandma Smith—both our grandmoth-ers, in fact—cooked huge meals without batting an eye. To a child, meals mark the day. How confused we were, when we visited each summer, that "dinner" was served at noon, sup-per was at night, and "lunch" was what we called "snacks." No matter their name, we loved the plentiful meals with their gravies and jellies and fresh bread and butter from my uncle's creamery. Even more, we loved the homemade—not "store-boughten"—cookies in the bottomless cookie jar: I still crave Grandma Smith's crunchy peanut butter and Grandma Short's moist sugar cookies.

But cooking for threshers means more than just cooking *a lot* of food. In our family, cooking for threshers means cooking *too much* food in the fear that there *won't be enough* and someone will go hungry. Is there enough? Will it make enough? Do we have enough? Enough, enough, enough. My mother is famous for buying too many rolls for large family gatherings, "just in case." The smoke alarm going off is a holiday tradition because she fills her largest scalloped potato pan so full of potatoes and cream that it runs over in the oven and catches on fire. Although she still makes twenty different kinds of cookies at Christmas, we've finally convinced her to bake double rather than triple batches. When you grow up cooking for threshers, it's hard to stop worrying about *enough*.

This "cooking for threshers" phenomenon seems to have been passed down from my great-grandmother's generation to mine. I've inherited the fear of not cooking enough at a meal, but as a child of the 1970s environmental movement, I counter my "cooking for threshers" fears with anxiety about wasting food if there's *too* much. Together, these influences are confusing. How much *is* enough? People certainly don't eat the way they used to, in part because no one today has the time to make everything from scratch, but also because most folks don't work as physically hard as they did in the past. Food today is plentiful, processed, and convenient, but contributes to obesity, high blood pressure, and diabetes. I doubt we even enjoy our meals as much as those threshing crews did.

Still, I miss the family closeness of the large farm gatherings of my childhood and the variety of food at every meal. I miss the Depression-glass dishes of homegrown and preserved vegetables passed around the table, platters of fried chicken, heaping bowls of mashed potatoes followed by the gravy boat, plates of bread and rolls, and angel food cake with strawberries and real whipped cream for dessert. Everything was fresh. Nothing came out of a box or tin can. Nothing went to waste, either. Those meals were truly abundant.

I think of all that threshing work—from the field work of the men to the kitchen work of the women—as "generative" work, the work that generates life, that keeps human beings alive from generation to generation. Our own harvests at Stonebridge are a descendent of my great-grandparents' generative work and our exuberant potlucks a reminder of delicious and abundant family dinners. Growing our own food helps me feel connected to those who only had themselves to count on for sustenance. If a crop failed, they didn't have enough. I like to think that John and I could grow what we need to on this land—even wheat, if we had to—but I know now that it isn't always easy. The generative work of growing and preparing wholesome food takes time and skill, but if we as a society forget where food comes from, we do so at our own peril. With all our conveniences, we still need to eat.

Great Grandma Flora Smith's World War II Victory Cake

1 3/4 cup flour
1/2 tsp. salt
1 tsp. baking powder
1/2 cup lard (shortening) or 2/3 cup sour cream
2 eggs
1/4 cup sugar
1 cup dark Karo Syrup
2 squares chocolate (melted)
2/3 cup hot coffee (or hot water)
1 tsp. vanilla

Stir together and pour into a 9 X 13 greased cake pan. Bake until a broom straw poked into center of cake comes out clean. Bake at 350 for 25 – 30 minutes.

This recipe may have come from the Royal Baking Powder Company, which published recipe booklets during the war. Many of the recipes of that time reduced or substituted other ingredients for butter, eggs, sugar, or coffee, which were in short supply or rationed for the use of the troops. Great-grandma Smith would fire up her big, black cookstove with coal and wood and then test the temperature by baking a little bit of the cake in the silver cover of the cocoa can because the temperature gauge on the oven door wasn't usually correct. Notice that the recipe is mainly a list of ingredients; cooks back then didn't expect such specific directions as we find today.

We sing along as Joe croons, "Kohlrabi just looks a little bit funny!"

Rockin' the Harvest

"It looks like you guys are having fun. Are you?" asked our farmer friend. We had just toured around our fall farm with her and her interns, discussing cover crops, harvesting the tops of walking onions for fall planting, and snacking on carob-zucchini cake made from the last of the summer squash. With only Brussels sprouts and spinach still growing above ground and root crops like carrots, leeks, parsnips, rutabagas, and beets waiting to be dug below, the fields looked orderly in their end-of-season garb. We always enjoy showing another farmer around the farm because we all learn from each other—and there's a lot to learn.

Her question took me by surprise. I had to think a minute, not because we weren't having fun, but because that wasn't what I thought we'd been emphasizing as we walked around the fields. She's an insightful woman, though, and she had cannily grasped that we do, in fact, always try to have a good time at Stonebridge.

"Yes, we are, we definitely are," I agreed.

"Good. Because so many of the other farmers aren't. They're working too hard, getting too big, and don't have time for the things they enjoy anymore."

I nodded. Getting too big is something we want to avoid. We've heard too many stories of farms gone under or split asunder from burnout, bankruptcy, or divorce. Especially divorce. Whether through necessity or habit, working too hard takes time away from the other activities that nourish us. The farm is not just a place of work but one of play where we sing around a campfire, jump into the swimming hole, or share a potluck meal. We love our work, but we need to balance it with music, laughter, food, and games because in life, as in farming, you reap what you sow.

That late October day was the perfect time to think about farm fun. All the winter squash and pumpkins were in the barn, one of autumn's biggest jobs, accomplished in relay fashion with our bartering members from field to truck and truck to barn. Most of the fruits, herbs, and vegetables I put up every season were in the freezer or root cellar awaiting our winter meals. Even the kitchen table was relatively clear—only a couple peppers turning red remained, while two weeks ago we could hardly find a place to sit down for dinner amid the drying seeds and ripening tomatoes. The most pressing fall work was done: cover crops were sown, alliums were planted. And we had just rocked the farm the Sunday before with a harvest concert by some of the talented musicians who are members here at Stonebridge.

Before radio, television, and iPods made music available beyond live performances, music making was at the heart of local culture. Communities worked, played, and celebrated with original songs of homegrown stories and their own versions of traditional songs that traveled with settlers across the continent. Local music beats from the heart of a community, especially in Lyons, Colorado, home to Planet Bluegrass festivals near the mouth of the St. Vrain Canyon outside our normally quiet town. From rock to roots, musical talent resides in every corner of our community, so what better way to mark another bountiful season at Stonebridge Farm than with a harvest concert?

July had been just plain hot—three weeks above ninety with no rain—and August brought the Folksfest and back-to-school preparations, so we hadn't yet gotten around to scheduling a concert. We talked first with farm members Jimmy Sferes and

Jen White of the Eco-tones, named after the space where two ecosystems meet. The Eco-tones' passion for music and a sustainable environment are evident in their performances and their original songs, like "Equal Shares":

Some things are for everybody
In equal shares
Like good clear water
And fresh clean air
Some food upon your table
And a place to lay your head.

Besides being local favorites who had played to many appreciative Stonebridge audiences, the Eco-tones have performed on *Prairie Home Companion*, at the Coop America Green Festival, and at environmental educational events around the country.

We suggested that Jimmy and Jen team up with Joe Kuckla and Emilyn Inglis of Coyote Moon for a Stonebridge harvest show. Joe had built the Sunflower Stage for our fifteenth season celebration when he had been the featured act. In fact, most of the buildings around the farm have benefited from Joe's considerable carpentry skills. Before Joe arrived at Stonebridge, our building projects fell into the category of what Joe charitably calls "farmpentry," a sort of "make do" and "good enough for who it's for" kind of carpentry. We've learned a lot from Joe since then. In fact, the "chickenhouse" would probably still be a chicken house and not a guesthouse if Joe hadn't taken it in hand, finishing the cedar boards salvaged from a plant nursery as paneling. He's even recorded some songs there that we jokingly dub "Chickenhouse Recordings."

Another of Joe's talents is extemporizing song lyrics that fit the occasion, like the time he wrote "The Grasshopper Eatin' Girl" about one of our young farm member's fascination with bugs. At our first homemade wine-tasting event, he adapted the words of his country love song "The Things You Do" from "I love you/ I just hate the things you do" to "I love you/ I just hate the things you *brew*." Joe also wrote "The Stonebridge Wedding Song" for our ceremony and we think it could be one of the most popular wedding songs around if word gets out (and we hope it will). Singing about love that grows stronger from season to season, the song captures the trials of both farming and relationships:

> *The summertime heat wave*
> *will dry out the land*
> *The plants will be crying*
> *out for your hand*
> *Your hearts will be choked by*
> *the weeds of despair*
> *But your love will grow with patience and care.*

When we finally announced the upcoming concert date, three of our other musician friends, talking in the fields while picking vegetables one Saturday morning, decided to throw a band together as a warm-up act. They had all played with other bands through the years but had never performed together. They chose a few songs, rehearsed in our Sunflower Community Room, and appropriately called themselves the International Harvesters, since together they represented Ireland (Ger), England (Peter), and the U.S. (Steve). True to their agricultural name, the Harvesters combined the wheat, chaff, and grit of classic pop with homegrown originals. Joe would join them on a couple songs and a surprise finale that would shake the stage and fill the festival field with, in their words, "an eclectic blend of Rock."

The October day before the show, the weather forecast warned of rain, but the next morning breaks bright and clear. As the crowd relaxes in view of Longs Peak and Mt. Meeker, the children play on the giant swing across the ditch and a red-tailed hawk soars overhead. The International Harvesters rev up the crowd with classic covers and Steve's original "Song Dogs," a favorite of the kids as they throw back their heads to howl "YipYipYipOwOooooooo!"

In contrast to the rowdy Harvesters, the Eco-tones take the stage for a mellow set with Jen's soulful, bluesy harmonies and Jammin' Jimmie's guitar virtuosity, finishing just in time for Jen to hurry off to introduce an environmental film at the local sustainability meeting in town.

By the third act, Coyote Moon, the clouds have started to gather, the wind kicks up, and a splatter of cold raindrops splashes the field. As the rain thickens, the less hardy of the crowd run to the nearby Sunflower Room where they can watch the show under dry cover. I hurry to the barn for rain-gear, which others don laughingly over clothes already damp from the cloudburst, but the hardiest fans keep dancing, their wet hair matted around their faces, spraying droplets as they swing and sway.

I'm barefoot in my long skirt, my feet cold in the muddy grass, a welcome cool down from my dancing heat. As Coyote Moon finishes their set with their own "Blazing our Destiny," my feet tangle with John's, he twirling left as I turn right, but we can't stop. "More, more," we cry, not ready to relinquish our rainy revelry. So Coyote Joe goes solo with slide guitar on his farm-inspired "The Things You Do":

Well I like spinach, red beets, and carrots
peppers and peas and chard
And watermelon
and a red ripe tomato
corn and beans and squash
Well I don't like arugula
And I can't stand those brussel sprouts
Kohlrabi just looks a little bit funny

A Bushel's Worth

But I like you
I just don't like the things you do.

In years to come, when Joe takes the stage with his band Crow Radio and their rock-boogie-twang sound, this song will still be a farm favorite. With its upbeat tempo and slide guitar, "The Things You Do" makes you want to country swing, which is just what we do in the wet field, singing along as Joe croons, "Kohlrabi just looks a little bit funny!" A rousing cheer arises from the Stonebridge fans who can appreciate the humor of vegetable lyrics.

Soon the rain lets up, just in time for Coyote Moon's encore, an Italian aria that highlights Emilyn's soaring soprano and Joe's rich baritone. By this time, the farm kids have dragged a picnic bench over to the swing to jump from a higher perch. They push off three at a time on the plank seat, holding tight to the ropes that extend thirty feet into the willows. With pretty good height across that ditch, as the music soars higher, so do they.

Suddenly, as the song approaches its ethereal climax, the youngest child accidentally slips off the swing and splashes into the middle of the ditch. The singers, oblivious to the side-show, keep singing in *molto voce*, but the audience holds its collective breath until the boy emerges, abashed but grinning from ear-to-ear. We laugh in relief as the aria rises to its transcendent pitch, filling the air with joy on this fall day. With the rainstorm passed, everyone comes back to the field for a few more songs and the secret encore to come.

Against the graying backdrop of Longs Peak and Mt. Meeker, the Harvesters take the stage again for a couple more songs, including Steve's original, "Holy Katrina," a satiric indictment of the Bush administration's calamitous response to the Gulf Coast disaster. As if in agreement, the wind starts blowing in the clouds once more, and a few folks start to pack up their things to head home. But the die-hards in the crowd, unwilling to let this last autumn afternoon end so soon, shout, "Encore!" until Coyote Moon and Jammin' Jimmie join the Harvesters onstage for a surprise finale, a rock and roll tribute that takes us back to the wilder days of our youth. With Peter on flute pitching a wistful opening, guitarist Ger backs up Coyote Joe on the vocal lead that builds, step by step, its own crescendoed stairway to heaven: "Ooooooh, and it makes me wonder."

Then, back on drums, Peter thunders the beats that propel the song from folk ballad to rock anthem, and the Harvesters, with Jammin' Jimmie on metal-bodied Resonator, blast a sound wave across the field to shake the fans of this homegrown band. Driving forward, the song modulates into final overdrive with Joe slamming Jimmy Page's famous solo, backed up by The Harvesters in blistering layers that pulse across the field to the farmers grinning before them.

Everyone is rocking as Joe pushes his straining voice further and further to "Stairway's" final hard rock stanza, ending with the cautionary words that remind this middle-aged crowd of what we feared most at seventeen about growing old: "To be a rock and not to rooooollllllll."

And then it's over and we're on our feet, cheering our hometown heroes and crying, "We're not worthy!" Our musicians have harvested another kind of crop at Stonebridge today. Like ten-year-olds who have swung themselves dizzily into the ditch, they beam from ear-to-ear at the cries of their biggest fans. For that glowing moment, in that autumn field with leaves blowing and friends laughing, we are again reaping what we have sown.

Packets of seeds lay hidden for years in the old Christmas box.

The Seed Box

Years ago at an antique show, I bought a square Victorian dresser box, about seven inches long in each direction, with a hinged lid and ornate brass clasp. Because the outside was papered with a green and red holly print, I thought it might be a special Christmas box for ornaments or jewelry, so I was surprised to find packets of seeds inside, carefully preserved like treasure in a chest. Here, a long-ago gardener had thriftily stored the seeds for next season's garden, reminding me of my grandmothers saving hollyhock seeds to plant next to the farmhouse for color against the green and gold of the North Dakota prairie. Like my grandmothers, this gardener may have been female, too, because the handwriting on the labels looks feminine in that careful, classroom penmanship of my grandmothers' time.

In the front of the fancy box I found five packets, much like they are sold today, in 2x3-inch paper envelopes colorfully illustrated with a vegetable or flower for quick identification: Scarlet Globe Radish, Tetra Snowdrift Alyssum, Purple Top White Globe Turnip, Danvers Half-Long Carrot, and some type of Bachelor Buttons, unnamed because the packet top was ripped away. These varieties are still popular today, but the packets in my box are from 1974 and cost only twenty-five cents each. The radish and carrots, in fact, were promotional giveaways from a Denver bank. "Grow with us in Colorado," the packets proclaim, although the seeds were actually grown for James Vick's Seeds, a Rochester, New York, company established in the 1850s. Vick had been a printer and journalist before starting one of this country's first mail-order seed companies; his catalogs were known for their horticultural advice and beautiful illustrations, some of which were sold as prints. Vick was also famous for developing distinctive flowers like white gladiolas, double phlox, and fringed petunia, types popular in turn-of-the-century cottage gardens.

James Vick might have been my box gardener's kindred spirit, sharing a love of seeds and the secret dormant life they hold, not just for the plants they promise, but for the shape and the feel of the seeds themselves. But most of the seeds in the antique box were not packaged commercially like Vick's seeds. Instead, they were carefully culled from my box owner's own garden or from the gardens of family and friends. Saved in envelopes, plain or airmail with their red- and blue-dashed border and winged "US Air Mail" logo, these homemade packages included marigold, columbine, cucumber, and scarlet runner beans, each packet with a different feel as I shook them. I save marigold seeds myself, so I know the feathery lightness of those slender seeds, wispy as butterfly wings. One of the columbine envelopes was marked "wild columbine," perhaps gathered on a hike in our own Rocky Mountains. Columbine is our state flower, so it is illegal to pick them in the wild, but I'm not sure whether seed saving would be a crime as well.

Tucked into a corner of the box I found two carefully preserved seed bundles, rather than packets like the others. One was wrapped in clear plastic and fastened with a strip of masking tape labeled "Balsum," with a "u," and underlined with a squiggly line. "Balsam" must be *impatiens balsamina*, or "Garden Balsam," an old-fashioned flower known for its colorful slipper-shaped blossoms. The plant is also called snap weed or touch-me-not because the seedpods disperse the seeds so easily, self-sowing the plant wherever they fall. My gardener may have collected the seeds in hope of planting them in a more precise arrangement, or perhaps a friend saved these seeds for her to share their cheerful blooms.

The other bundle, slipped into the very corner of the antique box, is my favorite: a soft wad of blush-pink facial tissue, taped and labeled "Pretty Ones Like Petunias Yellow-Blue-Purple." Preserved from the light, the tissue was still a vibrant pink, masking the seeds inside. I haven't opened the package but from the feel of them, I can tell they are not round and flat like petunia seeds, which are in the same family as tomatoes, peppers, and eggplant, but tapered like the seeds of a scabiosa or pincushion flower, each pod a small cone with fringed edges. But scabiosa, a member of the *Dipsacaceae* family, are certainly not like petunias. I have yet to solve this horticultural mystery.

Another question is their unusual wrapping. Were these unidentified seeds so precious to the gardener that she protected them in pink tissue? Or perhaps that was all she could find in her pocket the day she glimpsed the flowers growing in someone else's garden, surreptitiously plucking a few seed heads and hurriedly wrapping them in whatever she had handy to save and catalog for the next season.

A final mystery is why none of these seeds were ever planted, but stowed away in a fancy box instead. Did the gardener give up her flowers and vegetables because of illness? Age? No time to plant? Or did she abandon these saved seeds for more commercial varieties? Perhaps she forgot they were stored in the old Christmas box, certainly decades older than the seeds themselves. I owned the box for years, in fact, before I noticed the words "Flower Seeds" penned across the lid, now faded by sun and age.

Whatever the reason, I won't plant them either. Although I would not be surprised if some of the seeds are still viable, I would rather preserve this gardener's collection in their festive Victorian box as a record of her devotion to a garden long ago. When I take the box out each December to set on my antique sideboard with other Victorian decorations I have gathered over the years, the seeds seem content to have kept each other's company while waiting for their gardener's return.

Like this kindred gardener, I save flower seeds too, but mine are kept in old, oversized glass jars with vintage decals in the oak china cabinet I inherited from my Great-grandma Jacobson. Each time I plant flowers, I note the date on the seed packet and place them in the jars; at the end of the season, I gather all the packets, band together the empty ones with a label for the year, and keep the ones I can plant again the following season like zinnias, sunflowers, and marigolds. The banded ones go back in the glass jars—my seed archive—with the viable seeds stored in the cool, dry depths of my great-grandmother's cabinet until the next season rolls around. The packets record my flowerbed's evolution, year by year. A flowerbed is like a painting; the gardener selects for height, color, and flowering time to create a continual landscape of bloom. Looking at the packets again reminds me of the picture I was trying to paint.

Through the years, I've seeded penstemon, scabiosa, lupine, delphinium, coneflower, rudbeckia, poppies, forget-me-nots, sweet William, foxglove, marigolds, larkspur, cosmos, and nasturtiums—but the flowers with the most persistent history in my seed archive are *zinnia elegans*, the common zinnia. Although zinnias aren't the showiest of flowers, they are loyal bloomers in the late summer and early fall. Since I grow them for cutting, I have narrowed my selection to Benary's Giant, formerly called Blue Point. Every year I add a different shade to my mix of this tall, dahlia-flowered bloomer: Lilac, Salmon Rose, Scarlet, Lime, Golden Yellow, Carmine Rose, and Coral. The latest edition sounds like something you would drink on a Caribbean cruise: Queen Red Lime, with maroon outer petals around a lime center. But the flower itself has an old-fashioned appeal, like a silky mauve and chartreuse dress from the 1940s, gently swaying to "The Way You Look Tonight."

In September, our kitchen table is covered with small bowls of drying seeds. Because we grow only heirloom, open-pollinated tomatoes and peppers, we save our own seed each fall for planting next spring. Open-pollinated means that the new plant from the saved seed will come back with the same characteristics as the parent plant, unlike hybridized seed that contains genetic information from more than one parent and will revert to only some characteristics when grown from saved seed. By selecting several of the most perfect fruits from each variety, we ensure some genetic diversity within varieties and hedge our bets that each individual plant will be viable. In September and October, lunch means sautéing peppers and tomatoes for quesadillas, saving the seeds from each vegetable as we chop. And then we repeat the process each night as the fruit becomes that evening's meal, from stuffed peppers to spaghetti sauce. Once dried, the seeds are stored and labeled, ready for next year's starts.

As a seed-saver, I am following in the footsteps of other accomplished family gardeners. Over the years, my Aunt Del Vera has sent me seeds from her immaculate flower gardens, including her delicate pink poppies and double-petalled hollyhocks, saved in plain white envelopes, her exquisite handwriting underlined with a flourish: "Hollyhocks pink & rose."

My Grandma Short saved seeds too, not only flowers but vegetables as well. When I was growing up, Grandpa and Grandma Short visited each October after their harvest was finished but before snowstorms made driving from North Dakota to Colorado dangerous. Besides cultivating 130 acres of wheat and fifteen of corn, they raised vegetables for their own table, including two thousand pounds of potatoes each year. Every fall they would bring us our winter's supply of potatoes in a bag nearly as tall as I was.

One year my grandmother brought an immense, green winter squash as well, some kind of Hubbard, I'd guess, from its square shape. My mom could not cut it with her largest kitchen knife, nor could my dad with the meat cleaver, so he took it outside to split with an axe. *Whack! Whack! Crack!* It took him several tries before he could break its horny shell.

My mom joked the skin was so tough because my grandmother saved her own seeds instead of buying new ones each year.

It is true my grandmother's Depression-era parsimony made for some funny habits, but now I wonder about her seed saving. If the seeds were from a hybrid, the squash could have reverted to a harder-skinned variety that had been crossed with another for size or some other marketable attribute. Another possibility is that it crossed with another variety in the garden, since the genus *Cucurbita*, in which squash is found, readily cross-pollinates with others in the same species, and won't grow true to type. But if it was an open-pollinated variety, that squash may have been inherently tough, its hard shell a protection from adverse conditions. Whichever way it grew, it was delicious.

Today, many seed organizations and businesses are challenging the disappearance of "old-fashioned," non-hybrid, non-genetically modified seeds by saving historical varieties for future generations. The best known is The Seed Savers Exchange in Iowa, a non-profit network of gardening members who have saved over 25,000 varieties of heirloom seeds. In our own community, Abbondanza Farms is developing a seed bank of regionally specific seeds. These seed savers realize the inherent value of seed diversity for environmental sustainability, not just their commercial profitability. They challenge corporate control of seed sources because they recognize the vulnerability of an agricultural system that places fewer types of seeds in fewer peoples' hands.

Seed-saving is not typically a plot device in fiction, but in Joanne Harris' novel *Blackberry Wine*, seeds help connect the past to the present and extend a path to the future as well. As a boy spending his summers in a small English town, young Jay befriends Joe, an older gardener who tries to share his often inscrutable wisdom with the lad. This unconventional gardener saves seeds he claims he has collected on his travels around the world:

"In the big converted spice cupboard next to his bed there were millions of seeds, painstakingly wrapped in squares of newspaper and labeled in that small careful script: *Tuberosa rubra maritime, Tuberosa panax odarata,* thousands and thousands of potatoes in their small compartments, and with them carrots, squash, tomatoes, artichokes, leeks—over three hundred species of onion along—sages, thymes, sweet bergamots and a bewildering treasure store of medicinal herbs and vegetables collected on his travels, every one named and packaged and ready for planting."

Joe says that many of the seed varieties he's collected are already forgotten or even extinct, but Jay fails to understand the value of the seeds, wasting a gift the old man leaves before his sudden departure. Years later, Jay tries to reclaim the magic of those summers by planting his own garden in the French countryside. Though the connection with the past seems irretrievable, Joe's seeds—"hundreds of tiny envelopes and twists of newspaper, dried bulbs, grains, corms, seed fluff no more substantial than a puff of dead dust, every one marked and numbered"—are the gifts that save not only Jay, but the entire village.

What is a seed but a gift? A perfect package, each seed is, in fact, a tiny plant cushioned in nourishment and wrapped for protection. The Fedco catalog from which we order each year describes seeds as both "alive" and "dormant," a word that comes from the Latin *dormire*, meaning "to sleep." Without water, soil, and light to ignite their emergence, seeds rest. Patient in their dormancy, they wait for their chance to germinate and thrive. Until the moment of awakening, a seed can wait a long, long time. Once enlivened, they exist only briefly on their own sustenance, soon dependent on the earth, rain, and sun—or conditions that mimic them—to survive.

What's more a gift than a seed? Wildly diverse, seeds assure nature's treasure chest in miniature. Seeds are generative: their work is to extend the generation of plants and the world they feed. When the seed catalogs arrive each January, we order our future, choosing each gift with hope and delight. We spend our lives planting seeds, anticipating what will grow, and nurturing them until they flourish. For each variety threatened or lost, our chance for the future narrows. Yet planted once, a seed multiplies itself, guaranteeing the gift of its survival, as well as our own.

Our favorite apples—shiny green, yellow-striped, nearly black, and deep red with wine-tinged flesh—come from our older trees.

Appling

I'd been rolling apples down the chute into the grinder for hours, days, and seemingly weeks when I plucked one from the basket to consider its heft in my hand. *I hope I never see another apple*, I thought. *I'm appled out.* I couldn't even summon the taste I would so appreciate the next winter when I opened a jug or jar from this fall's pressing. Then I laughed and dropped the apple down the chute. My irritation passed as the spicy smell of the fruit promised the delight of Thanksgiving cider. The season had given us apples and we were appling.

My first semester as a college student in the late 1970s, I noticed the summer's change to fall like I never had before. Riding my bike to and from classes, the air felt sweet and cool. I was in a new town on a beautiful campus, enlivened by ideas and independence as the world opened before me.

One autumn day, I lay under an apple tree studying for my first biology exam. Suddenly, an apple fell on the blanket next to me. I didn't think of gravity, but rather of pie. I looked around to see apples on the ground, some rotting to the delight of wasps buzzing nearby, others half-eaten by wasteful squirrels. The light was cider-golden in the last warm rays of the season. I thought that a more perfect day could never be, not because of anything *I* was doing, but from the earth's creation of seasonal perfection. I noted the date, October 10, and most years since then I've remembered to observe that day's weather and light, almost always perfectly warm and golden in the sun's slanted glow.

A Bushel's Worth

More than thirty years later, I'm still noticing apples. Sitting in the flower garden, I hear an apple from a nearby tree hit the ground with its distinctive plop. The tree is heavy with fruit this year, although we have already picked as high as the bucket of the tractor will lift us. Our other apple trees dwarf in comparison to this giant, some intentionally, through horticultural selection, and others by age. This tree's apples are small but many, providing trugs full of fruit for pressing.

Red and Golden Delicious, Granny Smith, and McIntosh. Japanese Fuji or New Zealand Gala. These are the apple varieties you find in most stores today. Now look in the Fedco catalog and you'll discover Roxbury Russet, Garden Royal, and Newton Pippin, apples with fine New England heritages that have survived cold, hard winters. And on the web under "heirloom apple varieties," listing after listing of poetic names unique to particular orchards and regions appear: Brushy Mountain Limbertwig and Sweet Rusty Coat in Appalachia; Granite Beauty and Nodhead in New Hampshire; and Westfield Seek No Further in Massachusetts. Because apple seeds will not produce a new tree of the same variety—only grafted trees come true—at one time thousands of different kinds of apples were grown in this country for cider and cooking, yet today only a handful are available commercially.

But on farms like ours, folks are preserving older trees with names like Black Oxford and Fletcher Sweet. We don't even know the names of most of our apple trees at Stonebridge, so we refer to them as "the green apple near the outdoor shower," or "the nearly black apple by the maple tree." We have two old orchards on the farm, trees twisted and barren with age and neglect before John began pruning them back to life a few years ago. Now our favorite apples—shiny green, yellow-striped, nearly black, and deep red with wine-tinged flesh—come from these older trees. We may not know their varieties, planted before anyone here remembers, but we know they are special.

Apples are a treasured gift on this farm because most years the blossoms are literally "nipped in the bud" by a late frost. With global warming (or "season extension," as my old-time neighbor calls it, not willing to concede the political point), the trees flower too early, sometimes in March, and the new buds can't survive a late killing frost in May. But every three or four years, they either finish blossoming before the cold snaps or bloom later. Then the trees explode with fruit and we plan the autumn apple-pressing for the farm.

For years we used a small press about four feet high with a chute and grinding mechanism into which the apples were tossed and, with a turn of a crank, chopped into pieces that fell inside a foot-wide, perforated cylinder, where they were pressed with a vise until the cider ran clear through a lip underneath. We could press gallons of cider this way, enough for everyone to have a taste and take home a bit.

Then one year our friend Jon Bell somehow garnered an enormous old lard press, just the thing for apple pressing, he thought. Jon's an inventor by temperament but we call him "The Raven" because he's also a scavenger, showing up on our doorstep with someone else's useful discard. The machine Jon found is the Cadillac of apple presses; the cider gushes out the rimmed bottom and overflows into buckets that need frequent replacing as the wheel on top is turned by our members using a long stick through the crank for extra torque. I always imagine harnessing a small donkey to this machine, giving the children rides as the plodding creature turns the crank. But instead of a donkey, our members take turns in pairs on each side of the wheel, running in circles around the press as the cider flows into buckets beneath.

To complement this gigantic press, Jon Bell built a long wooden chute with an electric grinder attached at the bottom under a slot, a kind of bowling alley for apples that allows us to overturn trugs of apples at the top and guide them down into the hole, a perfect job for the mid-sized children who are old enough to be cautious about keeping their hands out of the grinder underneath. Even though Jon built a protective cover for the hole, we still worry about little hands getting too enthusiastic near the grinder, so at least one parent keeps a watchful eye on the young apple-chuters as the apple chunks drop into a bucket under the grinder. Four-year-olds, in particular, are meticulous about taking turns rolling apples into the hole so that too many apples don't roll down at once and jam the slot. "Your turn," they say, as they make sure everyone gets exactly their due.

Jon Bell also engineered a vintage steel water cooler into a cider-filling device by adding a narrow spout with an on-off lever at the bottom and covering the wide top with a fine screen to catch any seeds or stem bits that have escaped the press. With this cider cooler, we can easily fill the gallons and gallons of jars we've collected over the years for apple pressing. Still, we almost always run out of jars and have to scour the house once more for extra containers of any suitable type. We also ask farm members to bring their own to pressing events so that they're getting their "share" in their own jugs.

On a late September Saturday in an appling year, we hold one big cider pressing for our members. Anyone who comes and helps can take home fresh farm cider, but folks are also welcome to bring their own apples to press in the smaller press or as part of the bigger batch. We work for hours, taking turns at each task. Emily and Kunga sort the fruit while baby Osel chews on an apple, his grandmother Dhoka keeping a watchful eye. Renee, Jan, and Michelle wash the apples in trugs. Dave and Paul carry the trugs to the grinder. Marcel, Joel, Angus, Abby, Luca, and Grace take turns rolling apples down the chute. Eva the Elder changes the buckets as they fill. Hunter and Sarah lug the heavy buckets of apple chunks to the press. Mike, Jenny, Tim, Sandy, and Eva the Younger take turns at the crank, pressing the chunks into cider. John and Lloyd empty the crushed apples from the cylinder into the wheelbarrow to haul to the compost bin. Julie and Sarah pour the cider into the cider cooler, filling jar after jar with fresh juice. It's busy work that takes many hands, but anyone who helps walks away with delicious cider.

Besides pressing apple cider, an appling year brings lots of other apple delights. Apple pie, of course—great cooks will tell you the secret of a delicious apple pie is to use at least three different varieties of apples, blending sweet and tart. Dried apples, apple butter, spiced up or just plain, and apple chutney with cardamom, cinnamon, cloves, onion, garlic, peppers, plump raisins, and vinegar (especially one's own apple cider vinegar), served with warm Brie are farm favorites. Years ago some forward-thinking farmer put up gallons and gallons of apple cider in the root cellar under our barn. When John bought the farm, he discovered this stash of hooch, as we call it, and we keep it for special occasions to share with discriminating friends on Colorado's coldest nights. These apple gifts are reminders of how the things we need may just be "hanging around" the natural world, if only we take the time to appreciate them.

One year, after our apple season was over, I came across a book simply titled *The Orchard: A Memoir* by Adele Crockett Robertson. Books often appear to me serendipitously; somehow I stumble into their path when the timing is right, and the time was right for *The Orchard*. As a Women's Studies scholar who has taught life writing—memoir, autobiography, diary, journal, and letters—as literature, I was awed that the manuscript itself had been found by the author's daughter after the author's death. What a discovery! The story documented Adele Robertson's efforts to save the family's apple orchard as a young woman during the Depression. Her physician father had died, leaving a large debt, and the rest of the family wanted to sell the land. Adele, however, had learned the lessons of hard work from her father and wanted to keep the orchard. The physical labor required to prune, pick, and pack the apples with a minimum of hired help was unimaginable, especially for a college-educated woman of her time, but she did it without complaint, living alone in the farmhouse with her dog Freya for company. Not only did she grow and harvest the apples, she had to sell them, keeping one eye and a pistol out for apple rustlers. I won't give away the bittersweet ending, but Robertson's story of Yankee determination teaches us how a stalwart trust in the land and its providence can save not only a family farm, but also a young woman's future.

In *The Orchard*, I learned about apple varieties popular in New England at the time, from early pickers to late season keepers. After I finished the book, I got out my Fedco catalog and was excited to see some of the same varieties listed there: McIntosh, Baldwin, and Northern Spies, which, according to the catalog, may have been named after an abolitionist who helped slaves escape to the North. Adele Robertson also raised "Greenings," which were not as commercially popular at that time, given their green color. None of these varieties is quite right for our area, but McIntosh, a new apple in Robertson's father's time, has been developed into a second-generation apple called Cortland that's doing well on our farm. I'm glad to know that Robertson's apples are still grown in New England, a continuing gift from early farmers and the harsh northeastern winters.

My favorite Stonebridge apple tree grows on the edge of the old orchard near the flower gardens up above our second ditch. I never paid much attention to it in the past, probably because it didn't start bearing many apples until John pruned it over a couple winters. One fall I was standing outside the barn, talking to friends who had come to press their own apples, when I looked across the ditch directly at this tree. Its limbs were filled with burgundy-hued fruit, oblate in shape but not too small. I reminded myself to check on it when I had a moment, and soon I did. The apples were fragrant, not too soft but not too crisp. When I bit into one, I was delighted to discover its wine-stained flesh. Perfect, I thought, for pies, so I picked a few, combined them with a couple other varieties (following my "at least three types" rule for flavor), and baked up a mounding pie with a whole-wheat pastry crust infused with a bit of cider vinegar. When I took the pie out of the oven and cut into the center, I found that the wine-streaked apples had stained the pie a deep crimson pink, beautiful to behold and delicious to savor. I've tried to find the variety name for something similar to this apple, but so far, I call it "Stonebridge Sunrise" for the blush that veins its flesh like the early morning light. Now we've planted several that John grafted on cold-hardy stock in the hope of more pink-hued pies.

A couple years ago, after the farm season was over and the frosts had wrinkled all the leftover apples, I was walking along the bank, past the old orchard with my favorite tree, and into the overgrown, scrubby thatch where our property joins our neighbor's. Hanging from one branch off a tree that looked decidedly deceased, I found a single apple, obviously the remainder of last season's yield. The tree seemed to have mustered every ounce of energy to produce that one apple, just so I would know that an apple tree was still growing there, forgotten and neglected. Most of the tree is dead and a strand of rusted barbed wire, perhaps the remnant of an old fence, girdles the trunk, but that one branch is alive and promises apples again, when the time is right.

Excited to have discovered another old tree, I showed John, who will "prune at it," as he likes to say, cutting away the dead, gnarly branches and stimulating new, healthy ones. Given its proximity to the ditch bank, I doubt the tree was planted from a graft. Rather, the seed was probably buried by an industrious squirrel, so our tree is its own unique variety. Maybe next time the apples survive that late spring frost, we'll have another Stonebridge apple to try in our pies and cider.

Appling reminds me that the earth provides for our needs,

even the need for unbidden rewards, something we can't count on but instead must anticipate keenly. Our disappointment when the apples are nipped and blackened with frost is part of the lesson we learn, for our delight when the apples do come tastes all the sweeter. Appling teaches us to work together, to cooperate in our aims, for pressing apples requires teamwork with everyone playing their role, giving a bit more than we normally would. But appling can also offer a solitary delight in roaming the orchard, choosing the perfect color, shape, and texture, picking one apple, polishing it on a shirttail, taking that first bite, and smiling *yes, we are lucky*. In a good apple year, even the light tastes like cider.

Our root cellar reminds me of the colors of my grand-mothers' jars with their orange carrots, yellow corn, red beets, green beans and pickles, and golden applesauce.

Putting By

For years, we stored onions, pumpkins, and squash in the dirt cellar under the barn. The space is roomy and the squirrels and mice don't bother the vegetables much, but on a cold day, a trip to the barn isn't very convenient. Getting onions for dinner means leaving the warmth of the woodstove, putting on a heavy jacket and boots, walking through the snow, lifting the heavy door in the floor of the delivery room, climbing down the rustic ladder, carrying up the onions with one hand while negotiating the rungs with the other, and then hurrying back to the warmth of the house. The whole process made going without onions pretty tempting. Instead, we needed a space in the house for storing our winter vegetables.

In the days before central heating, old houses were cool and vegetables could be stored under beds and in closets. I like to imagine living side by side with pumpkins, potatoes, and squash, feeling their fullness in the autumn and eyeing their dwindling numbers as spring approached. Even though our old farmhouse is heated with wood and cold enough in spots for storage, our closets are filled with too much stuff to leave room for putting by many vegetables, although we always stash a few handy squashes in the closet of one of the colder bedrooms.

The root cellar project began when I suggested we insulate under the bathroom floor so that our first steps in the winter morning weren't a shock of icy tile. The pipes to our bathroom are accessed from a small room underneath with a door cut into the wall descending along the basement stairs. The little room's walls and the floor were dirt and the ceiling was formed from the joists of the bathroom floor above it. John had been thinking about that space as a root cellar for years, so, as we like to say at Stonebridge, the project had "finally come to the top of the list." When we helped our oldest daughter and son-in-law drywall their bedroom ceiling just a couple weeks before, we salvaged their discarded ceiling tiles, fabricated of wood pulp and painted white, for the job. John covered the ceiling and two walls with the tiles, encasing the insulation above. The dirt of the house's outer foundation formed the third wall; no fourth wall exists because the opening continues around under the oldest part of the house, but narrower there, more like a tunnel than a room.

Last came shelves: two tall ones for vegetable bins and one shorter at the top for home-canned goodies. Years before, part of the old foundation had collapsed in that space, sending two thick slabs of redstone tumbling down. John used those stones as the base of the shelves on the west side of the room. The lower shelves soon housed baskets and boxes of onions, potatoes, shallots, pumpkins, and winter squash, while the top was filled with gifts from friends: salsa, applesauce, wine jelly, and pickled beets, all shining expectantly in glass canning jars.

What a satisfying feeling to know that food is snuggled beneath us, ready when we need it on a cold winter's day, months before the next season's crops emerge. Our root cellar reminds me of the one under my Grandpa and Grandma Smith's farmhouse, with its damp basement and cool walls, and the colors of the jars with their cheerful contents: orange carrots, yellow corn, red beets, green beans and pickles, and golden applesauce. It's the colors I remember most, lined up in rows by shelf and type.

When I asked my mom what she remembered about her parents' root cellar, she wrote, "Mother had pickles, HA. She canned a lot of corn, and I helped her. They kept the potatoes and carrots in there. She canned a lot of beets. She also canned chicken and meat and lots of jellies." My mother's "HA" refers to her own pickle-making, bread and butter pickles from Stonebridge cucumbers or bought at her local farmer's market. My mother makes "refrigerator" pickles, not canned in water baths for winter storage but preserved with vinegar in big glass jars for fall eating, with a few set aside for Thanksgiving.

The root cellar on the Smith farm wasn't always there. My grandparents had the cellar dug when they enlarged the entryway porch, creating more room to shed muddy boots and heavy jackets in the winter, plus a storage cabinet for household tools, a coat closet, and a sunny window for houseplants. They moved the basement door too so that the stairs went straight down rather than turning awkwardly after the first few steps, making them safer to navigate. In the basement, they placed a heavy old wooden door at the entrance to the 12 x 12 root cellar that had been dug deep into the earth, the coolest place on the farm when we'd visit in the hot summer.

What a treat it was to accompany Grandma Smith when she'd venture down the steep, open stairway to retrieve a couple jars of green beans or some bread and butter pickles to fill the milk glass relish dish for Sunday dinner. Sometimes she called the root cellar the "cold room" and other times, the "fruit room." In the few diaries I have of hers, she often recorded the food she put by, even into her seventies:

Tues Aug 16, 1983: I baked 6 loaves of bread and we cooked and froze 12 packages beets for buttered beets.

Mon Aug 6, 1984: I canned chokecherries and made jelly.

Mon Aug 27, 1984: Nina [her dear farming friend] *came and helped pick cukes and beets and we canned 6 qts for her and 8 qts for us of beet pickles.*

Mon Sept 24, 1984: Made orange lemon and carrot marmalade.

A Bushel's Worth

As a child, I didn't think about the hours of work my grandparents spent growing and canning vegetables. Now I know—August, September, and October mean putting by the harvest and it's a lot of work. As I chop and puree and slice and boil during the autumn months, I remind myself of how happy we'll be to eat this food in the winter. I imagine pulling a handful of "sundried" tomatoes out of a bag in the freezer for omelets; defrosting roasted ratatouille for a ready-made candle-light dinner; or throwing frozen broccoli into a stir-fry with chard from our winter greenhouse and onions and cabbage from the root cellar. I'm not yet as industrious as my grandmother when it comes to canning, but her orange lemon and carrot marmalade is something I want to try someday.

The last weeks of the season, we begin to harvest with an eye to emptying the fields for the winter. We dig the onions and put them on drying racks to cure before storing them in the barn. If we've planted correctly, we have enough beds of leeks to give a bed each week. The same division works for carrots, turnips, and beets. We also start picking winter squash and give a different variety—delicata, spaghetti, acorn, butternut, red kuri, or carnival—each week; we'll offer a mix of what's left on the last Saturday's pick up. We harvest all the pumpkins, filling the back of the barn with our precious Winter Luxury pie pumpkins and other varieties for carving. We've got to get all the vegetables out of the ground, to the barn, and into members' kitchens before the season is over.

Every year around the end of August, the bartering crew starts to pick their date for that fall's first frost. These guesses aren't exactly scientific, but the prize is bragging rights, which are worth quite a bit at Stonebridge. With so much on the line, we need a clear indicator for the win, so we date the first frost as the morning we wake up to blackened and limp basil.

As the harvest hits mid-September, we keep an eye on nighttime temperatures. When a frost is predicted, everyone who can comes to "pick down" tomatoes and peppers like crazy. The tomatoes go on long tables in the greenhouse and the Sunflower Room to ripen; the peppers go in the barn for the next Saturday's pick-up. Our members get used to this pepper windfall at the end of the season. Too many peppers at once is a Stonebridge tradition, but at least they're easy to roast or freeze.

Sometimes it's early, sometimes late, but after the first frost is over, we will only be picking root vegetables—carrots, beets, leeks, turnips, rutabagas, parsnips, daikon radishes—and hardy greens like chard, kale, bok choy, totsoi, and spinach on the cool autumn mornings that remain of the farm season. The rest of the share will already be harvested and waiting expectantly in the barn.

When the first hard frost has come and gone, I take a walk around the farm to think about color. The day is overcast, making bright hues more vibrant than usual. Except for the gold of the aspens turning in the mountains, in Colorado we don't get the spectacular blaze that New Englanders would consider "fall color," so any flash of brightness stands out even more. The leaves have almost all fallen from the dogwood bushes on the bank by the swimming hole, their slender red branches russet now against the grass. Red too are the thousands of apples still hanging in the upper branches of our tallest apple tree. The fruit is small but sweet, especially after the frost. Yellow and gold patches of autumn foliage run along the tree lines of the ditches, the fallen leaves lying mosaic-like on the low surface of the water.

Out in the fields, the brightest color remains: a few pumpkins left to harvest, so large that we need a truck to bring them into the barn. They blaze among the wilting vines, reminding me of Peter Mayer's song "John's Garden." What's better, the pumpkins argue before Halloween,

A chance to shine
or die here on the vine?

But Mayer's song is too sad for me. I want both, the flash of fire in the fields and the glow of candlelight in the window.

In the same bittersweet way, I both anticipate and lament the end of the farm season on the last Saturday of October. I look forward to some quiet Saturdays in front of the fire, but I will miss working with our barterers and meeting our members in the barn. To celebrate another wonderful Stonebridge season, we hold our Halloween party on the last pick-up day, so the end of the season is a "trick" and the last vegetables are our "treat." We wear costumes, bring finger foods to share, carve pumpkins, and play donut-on-a-string.

We may be an organic farm, but on the last day of the season, we dangle powdered-sugar, white processed flour donuts in front of children's noses for them to bite and eat in one of Stonebridge's most venerable traditions. With five children lined up in a row and donuts hanging on strings from the official donut-dangler built as a school project by Eva, our young bartering member, the game begins. The children can't use their hands, so they stretch and jump and strain their toes and necks in the game, all the while unknowingly covering their faces with white powder. No one enjoys this game more than John, who laughs so hard we have to laugh at *him*.

After each child has played once or twice, the adults take their turn. Now the game gets rough, as the grown-ups in Halloween attire elbow, knock, and trip each other in their quest for victory. I always shout, "Work together," because if two people lean against each other, they'll provide mutual support and steadiness. But of course the real fun is in the competition as the adults leap treacherously at the donuts and each other until a victor emerges with a donut clenched between their teeth.

Another Stonebridge end-of-season custom is the "can-do" organized by Deborah, our recipe boss, who sends out a notice a couple weeks before the party announcing an exchange of homemade goodies. The rules are simple: bring one, take one;

bring two, take two. John and I usually contribute my farm photography cards and hand-cranked socks from his vintage, circular sock-making machine to the can-do, which stretches the "can" part a bit, but still fits the "do" requirement. In exchange, we receive jars of chutney, jelly, peaches, and sauces, as well as bottles of homemade wine, beer, and mead. Other people contribute home-baked breads and cookies made with Stonebridge ingredients. Many members bring an extra jar as a thank you to John and me for the season and we always appreciate those homespun surprises. The can-do shows off the talents of both the fields and the members; each year, our root cellar is amply stocked with their delicious gifts.

As some members play and eat treats inside the Sunflower Room, others sit outside at newspaper-covered picnic tables carving their Halloween jack o' lanterns. Every child who carves a pumpkin learns the discovery of its mysterious insides as they scrape the seeds and strings with a big spoon to create a shell. The custom began in Europe with carved and lighted turnips, potatoes, or beets to scare off goats and goblins, and was transplanted to the U.S. colonies when early settlers learned to cultivate pumpkins, indigenous plants of North America, from Native people. Today it's hard to imagine Halloween without the grinning face of an orange jack o' lantern.

Carving pumpkins reminds me of the Latin American *dicho*, or saying, *cada calabaza está el mundo*: each pumpkin is the world. A pumpkin is like the earth in miniature, round in its fullness and thick in its girth. Even more, each pumpkin contains not only the flesh to nourish us through the winter, but the seeds of a new world to plant each spring. From deep inside that seed comes the beginning of something both large enough to hold the future and bright enough to rival the sun. Pumpkins grow exuberantly, spreading their vines as far as the land allows. They need little care beyond planting the seed; nature does the rest. As a lesson in the fullness of farmgiving, carving pumpkins is a fitting end to a season of plenitude.

Autumn is a precious time. The sunshine is wavering and I'm drawn to the outdoors and the last remaining warmth. The rays of the fall sun are like saying goodbye to a loved one: each time you turn around, there's less of them in view. Every day of sunshine feels like the last, but soon we'll set our clocks back and the days will shift to a slower routine. We'll dig our sweaters out of the back of the closet, John will make socks in earnest, and I'll start plotting wool and needles.

After my walk, I go back to the house to check the tomatoes drying in the dehydrator and the huge pot of tomato sauce, flavored with red onions and colorful ripened peppers, simmering on the stove. Once I've finished cooking down the tomatoes left over from our last Saturday picks-ups, my putting by time will almost be over. The only task remaining is baking and freezing pumpkins and squash for winter soups and breads and, most wonderfully, Thanksgiving pies. But I'll wait for the season to end—and our Saturday mornings by the fire to begin—before I do that. For now, these ruby, amber, emerald, and topaz jewels are stored like treasure in the root cellar along the basement stairway, along with garnets and pearls of onions and garlic and a wealth of glittering canned gifts. Each time I visit the root cellar, I feel truly rich.

Putting by means admitting each season's inevitable fate, that the garden will wither and die under a blanket of snow and the transcendent cold will reign again. For a few frigid months, we'll harvest our food from the root cellar rather than the fields. But we are ready. Each year, as I place the last of the poblano peppers for winter stuffing in the freezer, I survey our stores and am satisfied. In the kitchen, I reassure John that we have put by enough food to get through the winter. He isn't worried. He has seen the work of the fields.

The last Saturday of October may be the official close to our farm season, but for me, Thanksgiving marks the true end of our farming year. Out of the root cellar comes butternut and carnival winter squash for soup and baking, onions for caramelizing, potatoes for whipping with butter and cream, and the root vegetables—carrots, beets, and parsnips—for a roasted root medley. We've left a little patch of leeks in the garden to dig fresh from the ground for the Thanksgiving meal. Those will go in the bottom of the turkey pan with herbs to flavor the drippings for gravy.

A couple days before Thanksgiving, I cook several aptly named Winter Luxury pie pumpkins for pulp and then spend the entire afternoon before the feast making pies. Of all the Thanksgiving foods, pumpkin pie, tauntingly spiced with cardamom, cinnamon, cloves, ginger, nutmeg, and allspice, is the part of the meal I look forward to the most all year. Home-cooked pumpkin is denser and thicker than canned pumpkin; with fresh eggs, the pies rise to the top of the crust and set firm and smooth to the touch. I always make an extra pie for leftovers, including breakfast the morning after.

Thanksgiving is both a celebration of the season's end and a promise of farmgiving to come. With our root cellar and freezer full, we gather in the knowledge that we've put by enough to sustain us through the winter. Other holidays have their special meals, but for me Thanksgiving is about preparing and savoring the bounty that the earth has provided once again. The season has brought us together at this table, expectant in the delight we are about to receive. As we share hearty squashes and rootful vegetables, we are reminded that the year's harvest isn't over but will be reaped through the dark months ahead.

But before the flurry of passing plates and bowls around the table begins, we recite a poem by Ralph Waldo Emerson to give thanks for the garden's goodness and another year of having all we need:

For each new morning with its light,
For rest and shelter of the night,
For health and food, for love and friends,

A Bushel's Worth

For everything [that] goodness sends.

And then we add: *We are thankful.*

Stonebridge Spiced Carnival Squash

Carnival is a colorful variety of winter squash that's particularly sweet and cuts nicely into wedges. If you don't have Carnival or an acorn variety, any squash will do if cut in 1 1/2-inch rings and then halved so the half-rings stand up in the pan.

Prepare spice butter:
1/2 cup melted butter
1 Tbl honey
1 tsp coarse salt
1/2 tsp each ground black pepper, dried thyme, cumin, and cayenne pepper
1/8 tsp each allspice, ground cloves, and ground nutmeg

Mix well and keep warm for drizzling.

Preheat oven to 375° and oil a 10 x 13-inch pan. Cut two Carnival squashes into wedges, inserting tip of knife into the top and following the grooves down one side at a time rather than trying to cut through the entire squash. Remove seeds and inner pulp. Stand wedges on their skin side in oiled pan.

Drizzle the warm spice butter over the squash. Pour 1/4-inch of veggie broth or water in the bottom of the pan to help the squash steam. Cover with foil and roast 1 1/4 hours. Be careful of steam when removing foil. Place wedges on large platter and drizzle remaining spice butter over the top.

Our tree was the oldest variety of cottonwood found on
Colorado's Front Range.

What Goes Down

For years, we dreaded the death of the venerable cottonwood that cast its meandering limbs across our irrigation ditch to the flower garden on the other side. Rooted on one bank, its trunk leaned nearly horizontal over the other, as if to form a bridge between them. The trunk itself spanned fifteen feet in diameter and was covered with a bark ridged a hand's width deep. Our arborist friend said such thick bark grew only on the oldest variety of cottonwood here on Colorado's Front Range, making our tree a hundred years old or more, following the digging of the Rough and Ready ditch in the 1860s, fifty years before our farm was established.

Standing upright, the cottonwood would have been the tallest on our farm. But as the tree aged, the weight of the boughs began to pull the roots from the eroding bank below, leaving less root structure each year to anchor the tree along the ditch's edge. The more the cottonwood leaned, the less water and nutrients could enter its system, and so the trunk rotted from the inside out, weakening the tree's ability to feed itself. As the cycle continued over the years, we watched the cottonwood tip closer and closer to the flower garden below.

But amid its decay, the tree was full of life. Birds sang and nested above, while squirrels chased their mates below. Raccoons ran up and down the hollow space inside the trunk, emerging on upper branches from rotted knotholes. Once I saw four baby raccoons perched along a limb far above my head. When I returned with a friend, five babies stared curiously from the bough; when we came back with yet another friend, six masked faces looked down as if to say, "See, they keep multiplying."

Despite such signs of life, we still couldn't deny that the tree was dying. When the hard winds blew in the spring, long branches fell onto the flower garden and into the raspberry patch, some big enough to worry about. We were tired of picking up deadfall, but removing the tree wasn't possible either, not without considerable expense and time to clear the remains.

To help lessen the weight upon the tree's remaining roots, we hired our arborist friend one May to trim larger boughs from the tree's north side where they seemed to hang more heavily. We thought that easing that side would help rebalance the tree and strengthen the remaining roots in the ditch. He pruned as much from the tree as he dared but feared that taking too much would leave too little for the tree's survival. Such pruning, we hoped, would extend the tree's life for many years.

May winds blow hard along the Front Range, hard enough to topple motor homes, overturn trailers, and push cars off the highway. Hard enough to blow water towers across the plains. Hard enough to worry about.

Three nights after the pruning, the wind howled and shook the house, but it didn't occur to us to worry about the tree. It had just been pruned, for one, and its mass still seemed indomitable. Barn roofs, yes, and the chicken house, yes, but that tree didn't even cross our minds as we listened to the wind shake the world.

In the morning, John went out to check for damage on the farm while I made a pot of tea. When he came in the kitchen door, I could see from his face that something had happened. "I've got some bad news," he said, but his next words surprised me. "It's the tree." Oh no. I waited, expecting him to say that a bough had fallen on the tractor barn or more scraggly branches had dropped onto the roses. That wouldn't be good news, but what came next was even worse.

"It fell on the flowers. It *covers* the garden. I don't know how we're going to clean it up."

In two weeks, we would celebrate Stonebridge Farm's fifteenth season as a community-supported agricultural farm with a pancake breakfast and outdoor concert. Friends were coming from out of state. John's family was arriving from Oregon. We already had lots of work to do before the big day. And now this.

I went out to survey the damage and didn't know what to cry over first: the crushed roses, the immensity of the work required to remove the branches, or the felled tree immutably spanning the ditch. No way could we move it. Even if the tractor were strong enough to pull it aside, there was no place from which to pull. We could remove the branches canopying the garden, but the giant trunk would have to remain.

Had our pruning unintentionally unbalanced the tree, shifting its weight on roots already vulnerable and weak? If the winds hadn't come so soon, perhaps in time the tree could have recovered its equilibrium, anchoring again more firmly in the bank. Our attempt to save the tree may have killed it, or at least hastened its end.

No human eyes had witnessed our cottonwood's grounding, the tree straining to balance in the fierce spring wind, giving in to the push and rocking to earth, the birds in its branches flying upward at once in the bough's final sway as the roots released and the trunk thundered to the ground, the impact so heavy it collapsed a metal gate trellising a rose.

But the Y of the trunk's main branches fell perfectly around the metal arbor under which we had stood when we committed our lives to each other. The arbor remained intact, the birdhouse at its apex hanging as before, the nest inside undisturbed.

For two weeks we worked whenever we had a spare moment, spending hours and hours together in the garden, John with the chainsaw and me in gloves pulling the cut limbs across the bridge to stack in a hundred-foot row six feet high, readying the remains for our friend's chipper. As we cleared the arching limbs and masses of small branches from the flower garden, we found other small savings as well. The stone rabbit wasn't crushed but cradled by two lesser branches fallen at its sides. Another trellis lay flattened on the ground but otherwise survived unharmed. We did lose the roses' last round of late summer blooms, but the plants would come back the following season and in future seasons, their growth more vigorous from the sun shining through the space where the tree used to stand. The trunk itself would make a naturally formed bridge for squirrels, raccoons, and children to scamper across.

And from the small ball of roots still fastened to the soil on one bank to the only branch left on the trunk at the other, enough nourishment is sent for new leaves to grow, a small but generative offering to the tree's insistent memory.

In yoga, we learn that when our bodies are rooted in the earth, we can reach for the sky. Rooted, we draw wisdom and energy from the earth and give it back again. I have been an intermittent practitioner for years, but lately seem to have found a more stable place for yoga in my life. Besides the benefits to my health—flexibility, strength, and energy—I have found that this practice roots me to Mother Earth in ways that complement the work I do on the farm.

As my teacher Lisa Limoge says while we kneel, stretching forward with our forehead to the ground in the child's pose, palms down, thumb to thumb, index fingers touching, and thighs cradling torso and organs, *let the great earth support your body and nourish you.* When I *come home to my body,* I can be like a tree, rooted below while drawing breath from above. With toes and heels planted upon the face of the earth, I will not fall off until my time for release has come. I can let go because *there's nothing to do, nowhere to go, no one to be.*

My yoga practice also helps me understand the impermanence of roots. In yoga, we witness the constancy of change and must accept that nothing in existence can remain the same. As Lisa reminds us when we're holding a particularly difficult pose for what seems much too long, *nothing lasts forever*. As our awareness focuses on the in and out of air filling and leaving our bodies, we relinquish the belief that everything now always will be. *Right now*, she says, *is a gift. That's why it's called the* present *moment*. But it won't last. Whether we're experiencing a moment of turmoil or pleasure, when we *move with breath*, change will come.

In my yoga practice, I struggle with balance. I can't always find the right position for my heels and toes to support me without wavering, without needing a prop to support my stance or weight. There are many *asanas*, or postures, that I can't yet maintain with grace and I wonder where my imbalance resides: my busy schedule, my resistance to change, my tense shoulders, my inner ear? Or perhaps it's just my fear that I will die before I accomplish my goals. I hope that practicing rootedness will teach me to accept the inevitability of impermanence, helping me achieve balance in my postures and my life.

One day in the mountains, sitting on a log by the edge of a shallow, sandy lake, John and I first heard, then watched, the falling of a towering lodge pole pine, one we had just passed under on our hike around the lake. No wind had urged its fall. Rather, its decline was decades in the making until it moved with its own breath, heaving its trunk to the ground, where it shuddered for seconds and then lay still. We wondered whether our footsteps had precipitated its descent, just as we had unintentionally hastened the collapse of our cherished cottonwood.

When a tree dies from natural causes, its boughs reach down to the earth as its roots are released from the soil and raised toward the sky. As yoga teaches, *what goes down must come up*. What first grew upward from a tiny seed must some-day fall back to the place of its planting.

Now when I pass the empty space on the bank as I walk to and from the fields, I try not to grieve the loss of shade that canopied my way. I've almost stopped mourning the cottonwood, accepting instead what's left. *Nothing lasts forever.* Above and below, before and after, we are always poised between different and the same. Only when we accept the passage from one to the other can equilibrium be found. Our old tree is gone, but with the sun across the roses and the trunk a bridge between, new roots find place again.

Flora and Jasper Smith homesteading on the North Dakota prairie with Myra, Lerah, Kenton, and my grandfather, Kermit.

Seeds of Never-Seen Dreams

On Thursday mornings at Stonebridge Farm, we work with a small crew of friends in the gardens, doing the tasks for which "many hands make light work." With this spring's cool weather and wet soil, I hadn't yet planted gladiolas, so one May morning I knelt in the clover walkways across the long flowerbed with two women friends, dropping corms into holes spaced three and then two across like cookies on a sheet. As we planted, we laughed about the patriarchal notions that had undoubtedly informed our feminism, ideas of women's subservience that seem as outdated as corsets and the Model T. The more we laughed, the more crooked our rows became. We recognized that the hard-won rights we once thought secure face vestiges of sexism still lurking today in our political system, but we also understood the determination of women not to return to those days. Trying to straighten our way down the bed, our conversation soon turned, as it often does, to stories of our families, or at least the pieces we know.

With the help of the alumni association at Valparaiso University, I had just found my great-grandmother's name listed in the 1890 Northern Indiana Normal School's catalogue under the Teacher's Department pages:

Hunsley, Flora   *Macon, Illinois*

Flora Delcina Hunsley traveled from Decatur, Illinois, at the age of twenty-two, to earn her teaching degree at the same school her brother Jake had attended for music a couple years before.

That catalogue is one of the few documents we have about Flora's life; the rest of the story can only be pieced together. At the Normal school, she became friends with Lola Belle Huckleberry, who had a stepbrother named Jasper Lemuel Smith. Although he was ten years older, Jasper and Flora met, courted, and married after she had taught school for a few years in Illinois.

My great-grandparents moved to North Dakota to homestead after Flora's brother Jake had staked a claim there. Her parents, Malinda and Charles, originally from the English county of Lincolnshire, went with them. Flora and Jasper raised five children, including my grandfather Kermit, on the Prairie View Farm. Their lives were typical of farming families, raising crops and livestock on the windy prairie.

But after their deaths, their children found their parents' secret in an old trunk: another document—their marriage certificate, dated one year later than the wedding date they'd always claimed. Flora had gotten pregnant before she and Jasper were married. After they left Illinois, no one but their parents and siblings were the wiser.

It's not an unusual story, but I wonder how Flora's life might have been different without that unexpected surprise. She probably would have married her best friend's stepbrother anyway, and, as a married woman, would have had to relinquish her teaching position, as they did in those unenlightened days when marriage meant pregnancy and pregnant women in the classroom wouldn't be proper. She probably would have followed her brother to North Dakota too, just as she followed him to college in Indiana.

But I like to think that she never entirely relinquished those days away from her family, going to classes, reading books, and finding a kindred spirit. When my aunt was born, my grandparents named her Lola after Flora's best friend. A college picture tucked into my aunt's baby book shows Flora seated with

Lola behind her and two unnamed friends at their side, proper in black dresses with jet-buttoned bodices, yet expectant with their dreams still ahead of them.

In Alice Walker's "In Search of Our Mothers' Gardens," she tells of black foremothers who, denied legal, economic, and political power, still told stories and planted gardens and pieced quilts of "powerful imagination and deep spiritual feeling." Walker writes, "And so our mothers and grandmothers have, more often than not anonymously, handed on the creative spark, the seed of the flower they themselves never hoped to see: or like a sealed letter they could not plainly read."

Even though I never met my great-grandmother, the choices she made were handed to me as I follow in her teaching and farming footsteps more than a hundred years later. But unlike my great-grandmother, I've been the beneficiary of a women's movement that fought for equal rights in employment, education, politics, and healthcare, changing social attitudes at the same time. As a young woman, I joined this movement and the sisterhood I found supported my choices as a single mother, graduate student, college teacher, and feminist. Once I became a farmer, I found another sisterhood with women drawn to the small-scale, local model of farming growing in importance today. Whether with male or female partners or on their own, women are creating new ways to be on the land.

My grandmothers and great-grandmothers were never called farmers. Even though they raised livestock and vast gardens to feed their families, even though they worked in the fields, made decisions about crops, and kept track of farm finances, they were called "the farmer's wife." "Farmer," in those days it seems, didn't only refer to the work that one did but to the gender of the person doing it.

Today, as farming is changing, so too is our idea of who can be farmers. Farming is no longer just about big machinery on big land or growing export crops for countries far away. With small-scale farming, farmers can build close relationships with people in their own communities, putting a member's or customer's face on food as well as a farmer's. This person-to-person contact is drawing women of all ages to farming, women who see a future for themselves in creating local food sheds and connecting everyone to the food they eat. Small-scale farming also allows women to include other traditionally female interests in their farming lives like cooking, education, and community service through classes, farm camps, and outreach projects.

As an educated woman raising her family on the North Dakota prairie, my great-grandmother Flora used her education to ensure her children's comfort and accomplishments, even in the difficult years of the Dust Bowl. Proof of her teaching skill is found in my grandfather, who had to quit school after fifth grade to take over the family farm. My great-grandmother continued to foster his love of reading and math, which helped him become a successful farmer. She never went back to teaching, but as she quilted near the coal stove in her later years, she reminded her granddaughters with pride that she had been to college. I think my great-grandmother would approve of women's choices a hundred years after she lived, new patterns for the hopes we piece together. Perhaps her never-seen dreams have become the seeds I plant today, stories shared between friends laughing in the clover walkways of the garden.

No one will suspect that the granary didn't begin its life at Stonebridge.

Keeping a Farm a Farm

I spotted one again last week: a subdivision with "farm" in its name. Land that used to grow food is now covered with beige houses. I don't know whether to take offense at the irony of a housing development named after a farm or take comfort that at least the name evokes its farming past.

The development pressure in our part of the Front Range is intense. More people moving to the area means more homes, more strip malls, more big box stores, and more light industrial and commercial businesses to supply jobs for the people who move here. And that kind of growth takes land. I don't know what the figures are in our county, but farmland along the Highway 66 corridor where we live is disappearing. I can't blame older farmers for selling their land to pay for their retirement, but it's heartbreaking that farms are rarely sold as farms anymore.

Still, farming today is a shaky enterprise at best. Costs are going up and the weather is less predictable, yet the physical labor required to farm isn't less demanding. John and I try not to worry too much about the things we can't control, but this season has been more challenging than others with record high temperatures, the threat of drought, and more deer eating our crops as wildlife comes down from the dry mountains to find food.

Last fall, the snow pack looked good, but March was warmer this year than usual, with no snow at all, dropping snow levels to fifty percent. I can't remember a March without snow here on the Front Range. We've always had snow in March, and not just snow but BIG snow, with many wet inches blanketing the ground. Sometimes, March snowstorms close schools and airports. On my fiftieth birthday a few years ago, the snow was so wet and deep, *everything* shut down. I even had to cancel my birthday plans for chocolate soufflé at our favorite French restaurant in Denver.

Front Range farmers depend on winter snows to come down the mountains and fill the reservoirs from which we irrigate the fields. We need spring snow to moisten the soil before planting and water the seeds while they germinate. With no snow in March, we were a little worried about getting the season off to a good start, so a little snow in April with a few stray flakes and misty rain the next day were welcome. Even better, the temperatures didn't fall low enough to hurt the fruit trees that had already started blossoming. Trees in bloom that time of year hold promise for an apple pressing. While no late frost seemed like something we should wish for, we know that record high temperatures in April signal a warming climate and more problems to come.

With the lack of spring snowstorms, agricultural experts warned that this year was the first of a three-year drought cycle and advised farmers to plan properly. We weren't sure what "properly" meant for us, except to water as much as we could while we had water, especially perennial plants and trees in the hope of getting them through the hot summer.

We have been through a drought before. In 2002, the irrigation ditch at our farm went dry. If it hadn't rained in mid-August, we might have lost our crops. We planted our vineyard that year and did lose many of the vines. Most people around here don't remember that we had a drought that year, but farmers do. Say "2002" and they know you mean "drought."

This summer we worried that 2012 could be that bad or worse—and if not this year, then the next. The grass near the barn looked parched before it had a chance to grow. We watered the fields in May as much as we usually do in July. We're luckier than others who don't have a ditch at all or who live further from the head gate and run out of water earlier in the season than we do, but once the water's gone, it doesn't matter where on the ditch you live. With record high temperatures in May as well, we wondered how we'd get through a summer that seemed to be starting months earlier than it should.

Hot, dry winds on my grandparents' North Dakota farms blow through my memories of our summer visits. Days are long in that northern state; to escape the worst of the prairie heat, we would run errands in town in the cooler mornings and spend afternoons in the farmhouse reading or playing games and drinking tall glasses of iced tea. Most nights, we lay as still as possible in our stifling beds as the sound of the fan whirring in the living room held hope of catching any small breeze through the open window until the northern sun finally set hours past our bedtime.

Summer heat evokes memories of the Dust Bowl, when farmland dried up and blew away, leaving fields unfit for crops or livestock. A consequence of years of drought and farming practices that overcultivated the soil, the Dust Bowl ruined many family farms that didn't have the resources to weather the tragic combination of severe climate, falling prices for farmers and rising prices for goods, government policies that favored large farms over small ones, and bankers telling farmers how and what to plant based on projected profits rather than farming know-how.

North Dakota author Lois Phillips Hudson's harrowing novel, *The Bones of Plenty*, depicts the agricultural, economic, and political factors that lead to one family's heartbreaking and inevitable failure as George Custer, a young farmer intent on introducing new practices, recognizes the problems inherent in old ways of farming but is powerless to change them: "And in the fall [a farmer] ought to leave the ground strictly alone, the way the buffalo and Indians left the dying grass to hold the sleeping soil in the clasp of an ancient root system while the winds blew through the fall and winter and spring." George is critical of older farmers like Will, his father-in-law, who plow the ground in the fall to save time in the spring: "[Will] had begun farming in the days when there were sizable stretches of unbroken prairie to help stop the dust, and like all other old men he figured that what had always worked should go on working." Faced with more problems than he can surmount, George wonders whether the days when a bushel of wheat could buy a pair of overalls will ever return. *The Bones of Plenty* testifies to the inept and greedy circumstances that exacerbated natural cycles and ruined family farms in the 1930s.

For my mom's family, the Dust Bowl—or the Dirty Thirties, as they were called—were both a terrible hardship and just another obstacle to farming on the prairie. My Grandma Smith, an immaculate housekeeper, always remembered how she couldn't keep her lace curtains clean because the dust blew in around the windows. My Great-Grandma Flora took in washing and ironing for railroad conductors and funeral home workers to help make ends meet. Despite the difficulties of the times, an entry on my great-grandparents' family in the local history collection says only this about those years: "J.L. Smith and his family survived the Dirty Thirties by working hard and taking care of the dairy cows which provided the family living." Sounds like my grandfather, their youngest son who took over the family farm—just work hard and you'll be fine. In his family's case, it was true, but my Grandma Smith's parents and siblings had a harder time and left their North Dakota farm in 1935 to become Idaho lumberjacks.

My dad's parents also left North Dakota in the 1930s for California, where my Grandpa Short pumped gas and my grandma raised my dad and aunt, who were both born in Sacramento. They did return to North Dakota after a year in Washington, eventually buying the farm in 1947 where I spent my childhood summers. In the same local history collection as the Smith entry, my Grandma Short shared a Dust Bowl memory of her father having to sell the beloved pair of Belgian horses he had bought for $1000, "undoubtedly the only money he had": "During the '30s the poor quality of feed wasn't enough sustenance for his prize animals. Dad shed tears and more tears as his horses were hauled away on a stoneboat. One of the results of the '30s."

These accounts of the Dust Bowl give John and me pause as our Colorado summers heat up. After we started farming in 1992, the hottest days usually fell in July and August, the heat broken by monsoon rains in the afternoons. But this year, May and June were the hottest on record, with five consecutive days in June over one hundred degrees, turning June into July, with few clouds to shield us from the sun's battering heat.

Every morning we checked our irrigation ditch for water. We received no official notice of an impending shutdown on our senior rights ditch, but rumors had us wondering how long we'd be able to water the fields. The first thing John did in the morning and the last thing at night was set the pump, watering for as much of the day as he could without wasting water to evaporation in the afternoon heat.

With little spring rain, new grasses and plants in the foothills and mountains did not grow rapidly enough to cover last year's dry thatch, creating quick tinder for lightning strikes that spread through pine-beetle killed timber. One Saturday afternoon in June, I went out to check the barn and ran into a friend in the flower garden who had just picked up her weekly share. She was looking to the north and pointed to a plume of smoke. "There's a fire north of Fort Collins," she told me. "It looks bad." We stared at the black smoke, knowing how dry the land had become this spring and worrying about how quickly a fire could spread.

Started by a lightning strike on a beetle-killed pine tree that smoldered for several days before collapsing and igniting dry grass, the High Park fire blazed for three weeks, destroying 259 homes and 87,000 acres of beautiful forest land in three different northern Colorado canyons. Each day, we could see the plumes from our farm and smell the smoke, a daily reminder to use precaution in all we did, like reminding farm visitors not to smoke anywhere on the farm and watching machinery for sparks that might ignite dry grasses.

Then one morning we woke up to thicker smoke hanging in the air, and we knew the fire we'd heard about in Estes Park, a small mountain town twenty minutes up the canyon from our farm, had worsened. That fire started in a housing subdivision near the southern entrance to Rocky Mountain National Park, close enough to threaten western parts of the town. Four thousand three hundred people, including patrons at our favorite Estes restaurant, The Rock Inn, were evacuated the first night; horses from nearby stables were relocated to the fairgrounds. Throughout the morning, the smoke seemed to shield us from the intense heat of the sun as the temperature neared one hundred. Thankfully, the fire was out by late afternoon, but not before twenty houses burned to the ground. A young firefighter went out on her first call with that fire—to her own family's home.

Other fires followed, including one in the Boulder foothills. Visiting friends the night after the fire started, we could see the flames along Flagstaff Mountain, a smaller fire damage-wise but still frighteningly close to outlying homes and the city itself. With all these fires, even rainstorms were a mixed blessing since hot winds could whip the fire up and lightning could ignite a new blaze in the tindered land. It wasn't until temperatures cooled and the monsoon rains came in July—a month that normally brought our highest temperatures—that the fire threat abated, but not until after thousands of firefighters had battled up and down the Front Range for weeks.

With fires raging across the western United States, environmentalists like Bill McKibben warned that, amid rising global temperatures and their attendant increase of heat on the earth's surface and atmosphere, weather extremes like the summer of

2012's are "the new normal" that we can no longer ignore. At Stonebridge, we noted the impact of the warmer temperatures on our crops: spring spinach and lettuce bolting earlier than usual; smaller heads on broccoli and cauliflower; difficulty germinating beets, carrots, and green beans; tomatoes failing to set blossoms in June; and, one benefit of a longer hot spell, larger onions than we've ever harvested before. We also had zucchini, to quote our friend Joe, "like you wouldn't believe." With the warm spring, John planted it a month earlier than usual and then replanted at its normal time just in case the first planting failed to thrive. Our members were asking for mercy; we couldn't even give zucchini away to our local food pantry because everyone else had too much zucchini too.

The summer went on, hot and dry, while we tried to anticipate what we should do next. Apples and raspberries were ready early. Would the wine grapes in our vineyard ripen ahead of schedule too? We abandoned the stifling upstairs room in our old farmhouse and quit checking the weather report, figuring "Hot" was in the forecast and we'd rather not know how hot "Hot" would be.

And then it rained. Not just a few drops to sprinkle the arid earth—a real rain that brought much-needed moisture to our area.

But that sounds like a weather report. Here's what really happened:

When the rain came, I was playing old-time music on the back porch of our Sunflower Community Room. We gather there once a month to share three hours of old-time groove with a revolving group of dedicated, experienced, and aspiring musicians. I'm not much good on the mando yet, but I know when a song really moves, when the music seems to find itself in the rounds of repetition, part A following part B, whirling us away in merry abandon until someone lifts their foot to signal the last go-round.

A Bushel's Worth

We were playing out on the screened porch, trying to catch any breeze a breathless evening offered, when we glanced an unanticipated flash of lightning strike west of the farm toward Longs Peak. I hadn't checked the weather report, having conceded the inevitability of many hot July days to come. With June temperatures the hottest on record since 1977, and May and April similarly record-shattering in terms of heat, we'd been so many weeks without a real rain here, even the possibility of rain had grown dim. After only a few slight showers in the last two weeks brought little rain but many lightning strikes to start some of Colorado's worst fires, any sign of lightning was sobering. I've lived here long enough to know that lightning near Longs means a storm is on its way. Still, a real storm didn't seem particularly imminent.

I don't remember which tune we were playing when the rain came. John says it's all the same song anyway, and he's got a point. Old-time music draws on endless variations of melodies within a given key, but the fact that each is named and remembered proves their distinction. The names themselves are part of the music's charm: names like Bear Went Over the Mountain, Sally's Got Mud, Sweet Milk and Peaches, Run Down Boot, and Squirrel Hunter portray the down-home, feel-bad feel-good sense that playing old-time brings.

Perhaps we were playing Garfield's Blackberry Blossom, a traditional song that pre-dates that president (a relatively newer "old-time" song, Nixon's Farewell, commemorates another). And then the wind picked up, blowing one strong gust through the porch that sent me flying into the community room to shut doors and windows before the tablecloths were thrown askew or worse. Still, I didn't think the storm would amount to much and went back to the circle to join another round.

When we were knee-deep in the next tune, the rain began, barely a few drops falling before the thick clouds opened over Stonebridge, pounding the tin roof over our heads. When lightning cracked above us, we raised our eyebrows, glancing first at each other and then outside at the dimming light, but without skipping a beat, kept our groove as the rain poured down around us.

Which would finish first, the song or the storm? Another flash of lightning decided the point. The rain had more staying power than we did. As we finished the tune, we turned to each other, surprised at what we'd come through. "We brought the rain!" we cheered. A real rain. A cloudburst. A thunderstorm that promised more to the fields than anything we'd seen in months.

The rain poured for ten minutes and left puddles in the ruts of the driveway outside. A few people left to get home before dark and a few more arrived with umbrellas. As we began another tune, the wind blew cold air across the porch. After so many weeks of heat, it felt good to be chilled—until it didn't, and we moved inside to finish the evening with a few final old-time tunes.

As we left the Sunflower Room with our instruments, the nearly full moon filled the puddles in the road with light. The night breeze hummed the storm's exuberant passing, a melody of moisture replenished, crops revived, and farmers and musicians refreshed.

The next morning, the farm looked different: fresh, verdant, and relieved, like it might make it through the season after all. To celebrate the rain, I transplanted mint under the outdoor water spigot at our farmhouse. That's where my grandmother kept her mint on the North Dakota prairie, the only place it was guaranteed moisture; when she'd water the flowers along the side of the house, the spigot would leak onto the mint. She'd make tea from that mint, the coolest drink of the hot summer.

The smell of mint reminds me of my grandmother and the childhood summers I spent on the farm. My grandmother didn't waste water. She even washed dishes in a tub in the sink so that she could throw the water on the flowers when she was done. Given the fires and drought of this summer, planting mint under our own spigot seemed like a hopeful tradition. The hottest months weren't over and our ditch could run dry yet. We were still worried about a warming climate changing our weather patterns and impacting the way we farm, but that morning, we were happy for the reprieve of a rainstorm and the return of green.

Yelling. I hear yelling. Why would someone be yelling at this time of the morning? Maybe it's those kids next door, but I wouldn't think I could hear them from the house. It's not John. He's out in the field. I just saw him there fifteen minutes ago. I've only been inside a couple minutes. But I still hear it. Who is it? Is it him? Maybe I better go look. I'll just listen out the back door.

It's stopped now. I wonder if John heard it. I think I better check on this. I'll walk back and ask him.

I walk over the stone bridge, past the barn and greenhouse and around the corner of the Sunflower Room. There he is, sitting on the ground by the front wheels of the red tractor. He must have come back to the tractor barn to fix a tire.

"Hey, did you hear yelling?"

He turns to me with a strange, stunned look on his face. "Yeah, it was me. . . . But I'm not hurt."

"Oh my gosh. What happened?" I see now that he's sitting awkwardly on the ground. Did the tractor roll over his legs? Is he trapped? Am I strong enough to lift a tractor?

I run toward him and am thrilled to see that his legs are fine. What's the matter then? What else can it be?

John's voice is hoarse but calm. Still, I can see he's shaking. "My hand's stuck but I'm okay. I'm trying to get it out. The jack fell and my finger got caught in the wheel."

The tractor's not on top of him. That's good. I put my hand on his back. He's trembling but he doesn't look like he's going to pass out. I glance at the wheel and I don't see blood. We can get his finger out. There must be a way.

I think I should call 911 but I'd have to run back to the house and that would take time, so I make my voice as steady as I can. "Okay. What do I need to do?"

John's got a plan. When he thought I couldn't hear him yelling, he figured out another way to get free. "I was going to have you lift the tractor with the jack but I don't want it to slip again. I think I can jimmy the hub away from the rim with the wrench. My wedding ring stopped them from crushing my finger."

I can see now that his left hand is wedged between the tire rim and the heavy steel hub of one of the tractor's front tires. His ring is caught between them but his fingers are intact. With the wrench he'd been using to change the tire in his right hand, he's pushing the rim away from the hub. He twists the wrench hard against the steel to lift the rim away, just enough to slide his hand out and, suddenly, he's free.

"It's okay. I'm okay." He hugs me and I cry a little, a few sobs to shake off the fear pooled in my body. Then I look at his finger. His ring has gashed into the skin above but the cut is not very deep and hasn't drawn much blood.

"Let's clean it up and see if it needs stitches," I advise. Later, we'll figure out what to do about the tractor. For now, we walk back to the house slowly, arms around each other, shaking and scared at what could have been, but thankful at what wasn't.

John's finger will heal. My heart will stop pounding each time he goes out to the field. Peter and Deirdre will buy John a whistle that hooks onto the belt he wears with his other tools, accompanied by Peter's sonnet that ends:

To summon aid no need to write epistle
Inhale like Zeus and blast the orange whistle.

We threaten to take that whistle away again when John blows it on Saturday mornings to get our attention amid garden chatter, but we won't. Farming is dangerous and one never knows where the hazard may lie. In a life of constant risk, each small protection counts, a steady reminder to be safe, take precautions, and keep our eyes and ears open for each other.

Out on the prairie, east of Stonebridge where our highway meets the interstate, a granary sat empty for years. Granaries are structures for storing grain, in this case a wooden building once filled with wheat through a door in the gable. Where I'm from in North Dakota, "granary" is pronounced "grainery," but there "threshing" is called "thrashing" and a "creek" is a "crick," too. I prefer the older pronunciation, with "an" like "grand"; it lends elegance to the building's simple construction and mundane use. Today, grain elevators have replaced farm granaries but many still dot the countryside in this part of the country. You've probably passed one without even noticing.

At Stonebridge, we like making old buildings useful for our needs as a small community farm. After renovating the few built here a century ago—the chicken house turned guesthouse, the hog barn turned community room, the farmhouse refurbished, the barn repaired—we were looking for another old building to restore. We wanted sleeping quarters for friends to visit and writers to retreat, so we asked our friend and scavenger extraordinaire Jon Bell to keep an eye out for us. On one of his jaunts out east, he found the granary on an abandoned farm site sold for a development that hadn't yet reached the eastern edge of its forty acres. The houses are coming its way, though, and we thought we might as well move the granary to our farm than let it be bulldozed for subdivision sprawl. Jon found the owners living down the road and asked their permission to take the granary to a new home at Stonebridge. They'd bought that old farm at the edge of the highway a couple decades earlier to try their hand at farming and raising hogs. But as the edge of the city moved closer, they were ready to sell when the right offer came through.

The granary sat empty for years, but it isn't the worse for

wear. The building houses three rooms: a center room for storing grain; a small side area with a ladder for checking the grain at the top of a wall that doesn't quite reach the ceiling; and a larger storage room on the other side with a chute near the floor on the inside wall for filling grain bags. Besides the door in the gable through which grain could be poured into the center room, the building has an outside door to the storage room and a small door into the space with the ladder. Despite sitting unused for years, the building is clean. We found some grain sacks and a wooden box, a little dust, and some old lumber, but no graffiti, empty beer bottles, or cigarette butts. Besides a few mice making their nests, no one has been up to mischief there as far as we can tell.

On cold, windy days in February and March, John, Joe, and Peter spent hours removing the roof shakes and rafters so that the building would be low enough to fit under wires as it came down the highway on a flatbed trailer. While they were at it, they took down two hundred feet of old board fence as well, using some of the pieces to panel the outside of the "bluehouse" they reconstructed this winter for growing the spring's lettuces and next year's winter greens. They'll use the lumber to rebuild the granary on its new site at the edge of our meadow too. You can't buy wood like that anymore, fine-grained and strong without chemical toxins, sounder and safer than the lumber euphemistically called "pressure-treated" today. A couple of the boards may even become a guitar someday.

Roof and beams removed, the granary left its original home last week to make its way down Highway 66 toward the foothills for its new life at Stonebridge Farm. The team jacked the building up on old beams four feet high to allow clearance for the thirty-foot-long trailer. The young man we hired to move it down the highway slipped the trailer underneath and belted the building from top to bottom, making sure each chain or buckle fit snugly around the frame. It was as wide as legally possible without requiring a special permit and, we would soon find, as wide as would fit through the space between buildings on the road at our farm. With the old building secured to the trailer, John and Jon loaded the extra beams into their trucks for lowering the granary at its new Stonebridge site. And then, we were ready to shivaree it down the highway.

Which didn't take long. A granary on the back of the trailer didn't slow that truck down. I stopped for a picture of it coming west towards me on the highway but had to jump back in the car and speed to pass it in the only multi-lane stretch so that I could catch another shot turning onto the farm. I don't think anyone on the highway gave the granary a second thought, if they noticed it at all. Just an old wooden building coming down the road, not a piece of history moving from times past to a new home in the future.

Our young trucker started driving machinery on his family's farm at age nine but had never moved a building like our granary before. Nor had he navigated his trailer through such a narrow path as between our barn, community room, and glass greenhouse. He even stopped a couple times to take pictures of how tightly it all fit. But by pulling a few fence posts and turning up the corner of a metal roof just in case, he got granary and trailer through without a scratch. We all breathed a sigh of relief when he pulled the trailer out into the wide meadow, hauling the granary as close as he could to its future site. The crew stacked timbers underneath as the trailer moved out and then jacked the whole thing down onto longer beams newly milled for the foundation. As soon as he can, John will pull it on chains with the tractor to its proper angle facing the meadow.

The granary doesn't look like much right now without a roof or proper windows or doors. In time, we'll clear it out, hose it down, rebuild the roof, remove the low wall, cut another outer door, add some windows and a porch, insulate the walls, and paint it white like it used to be. I think it will be prove a quiet space for writers and friends to relax and work and listen to the birds in the old willows along the ditch at the edge of the meadow. No one will suspect that it didn't begin its life at Stonebridge, although they might wonder why there's a door in the gable. We'll leave that, evidence of its former purpose, to remind us how close we all once lived to our food.

We may have preserved the granary, but the farm that the granary sat on could not be saved, and that is a shame. Once farmland is developed, it won't be farmed again. That loss affects all of us, not only in the lack of food raised locally, but also in the demise of natural habitats for plants and animals. Harder to measure is the degradation of the human spirit as the natural world vanishes from our collective imagination. While the domain of wilderness exists as a world literally outside our human dominion, the cultivated space of farming provides an affiliation with nature alongside our human stewardship. Both wild and cultivated spaces must be preserved, for without them, we will mistake our desire for the artificial products of our society for our reliance on the real substance of our planet and, in doing so, seal our fate. Perhaps we already have.

At least in our area, the county itself is interested in preserving farms and has purchased thousands of acres as agricultural open space. We disagree with the county over the allowance of GMO crops on public land, but we are glad the county is far-sighted enough to create a new "rural preservation" designation under which our farm now falls. That means the land can't be developed for industrial or commercial purposes, at least for the next ten years and hopefully beyond.

John and I are still in our fifties and, barring illness or injury, plan to farm for many years to come. But we are starting to take steps to ensure that Stonebridge remains a working farm—not a housing development called "Stonebridge Farm." We're teaming with our local officials to foresee and guarantee options down the road such as land conservancy and open space acquisition. And this summer we welcomed the birth of our first grandchild who may—we hope—want to farm someday. Still, we know we are the ones who have to preserve Stonebridge now if the farm is to survive. It's sad to think we won't be here forever, but even sadder would be the loss of this land to asphalt and concrete.

Every spring for the last twenty-some years, we've started seeds in the greenhouse and transplanted them into the fields. With the help of our dedicated friends, we've watered and weeded and waited each day until the harvest is ready. And with the support of a loyal community that understands the importance of local agriculture, we make it through another season. Only that kind of care and commitment will keep Stonebridge from becoming another subdivision with "farm" in its name.

Some friends of ours got married this summer in a beautiful ceremony on a serene lake in the middle of farmland not far from Stonebridge. Watching our friends vow to grow in understanding and support of each other as they unite their hearts in love and partnership, I thought about how marriage and farming are alike. Most apparently, both marriage—in whatever form it takes—and farming require a deep, long-term commitment to someone or someplace other than one's self. Without a commitment to the future, most of us would hesitate to take the risks needed for continuous growth. Commitment acknowledges that relationships, like farm seasons, will encounter bad times with the good, while depending on mutual dedication to endure the challenges that inevitably arise amongst the pleasures.

Marriage and farming are also alike in that both demand constant attention to the ever-changing aspects that influence our day-to-day acts and projected goals. We must stay engaged with the other to make the best decisions toward our mutual benefit, bringing a mindful openness to whatever changes arise. All relationships are influenced by outside factors beyond our control. In the case of farming, these are literally outside, since the natural elements determine so much of what we do. Like marriage, farming requires that we respond to the nuances of our environment and the needs of the something or someone outside ourselves, a never easy task amid the busyness of our lives.

But like farming, in marriage we also experience moments of balance and bliss where we can enjoy the fruits of our labors and rest upon the actions already taken. This stasis, however temporary, helps us recall why we have committed our best selves to something beyond our individual desires. Those moments come in all sizes, from a quick smile on our way out the door to a romantic getaway, from looking back at a well-weeded bed to a harvest concert in the autumn sun. Those are the times we stop to remember: *This is why we do what we do. This is what our hard work brings. This is the moment for which we have come together.*

For John and me, our combined commitment to each other and to Stonebridge—the land and the community—keeps us farming. This record-breaking summer brought more new challenges than most with its own successes and failures. The early crops suffered from the heat, but we gave our members peaches from our own tree for the first time ever. Bags of giant onions waiting in the barn will soon be joined by a succession of bright winter squashes now ripening in the fields. By season's end, we'll bring in more than enough food for our members with extra for the food pantry to provide needed meals to families in our little town.

On a farm, all this generative growth holds another kind of promise, one specially transacted between farmers and the earth. If we do our best for our part—planting, watering, weeding, thinning, and harvesting—the soil, water, wind, and sun will do the rest. I think we get the better end of the deal.

As we face a future that looks a little different than we expected more than twenty years ago when we started farming here, we hope that fulfilling that promise on this piece of land will still make sense. Will farming on a heavily developed corridor across the highway from an eight-hundred-acre housing subdivision still be desirable? Or can we avoid that kind of unchecked growth through progressive planning policies that value rural preservation to keep a farm a farm? We hope so. This challenging season has shown us once again the leap of faith that farming requires: we never know what we'll harvest until it is time to reap. As we finish one season and plan for another, we'll work with our community toward ensuring the farm's future, fertile and full for the growing.

The old mailbox from the Short farm waits in the rose garden for a letter or a bird to make a home.

Salvage

Granary, shed, tractor, truck, plow—that was the stuff of my grandfathers' farms. My grandmothers' farms were found in smaller objects—breadboard, coffeepot, and bottles of Ivory Liquid to wash the interminable dishes. For years before she had indoor plumbing, my Grandma Short had to draw water into a dishpan from the big red pump in the kitchen. Grandma Smith had running water out of a faucet, but still washed her dishes in a dishpan so she could throw the water onto the flowers when she was finished. From my grandmothers I learned the lesson "Waste not, want not."

My grandparents farmed in North Dakota during the Depression and WWII when money and materials were scarce. Even after those hard times were over, they never left that thrift mentality behind. Grandma Smith extended her diaries an extra year or even two by filling in the leftover spaces: "Never wrote here last year," one entry remarked. Grandma Short saved wrapping paper and old jars in closets under the roof's eaves.

Although I never heard them say it, the WWII slogan "Use it up, wear it out, make do, or do without" describes their frugal rural ways, but their thriftiness was a habit born of self-sufficiency rather than parsimony. Trips to town take time away from farming, so it was better to save what you had to use again rather than have to buy it new. Any little piece of wire could come in handy for fixing a broken fence or lock; that leftover jar might be just the right thing for jam or pickles. Buy in bulk and stock up on sale so that you don't have to run to the store. Grow your own food because it tastes better than what comes out of a can or box. Make it yourself with what you have and you'll be happier in the long run.

When John bought Stonebridge, he found the previous owners had practiced the same kind of thrift. In the tractor barn, handmade drawers hold hundreds of old nuts and bolts that have come in handy more than once. My own "make do" inheritance is most obvious in my hesitance to throw away a glass jar with a tight-fitting lid. I look at it, thinking, "What could go in this jar?" and I imagine the day I'll need just that size as I stack it on a long shelf in the basement pantry. Boxes, too. I can't stand the thought that I might not have the right box handy when I need to mail something right away, until the pile gets too high and necessitates a trip to the recycling center. I was horrified one day to find a new kind of soap that doesn't have a center because, the company claims, that part goes "unused." They're wrong about that, at least on our farm. I love using the hard little middle of the soap until it's gone.

Raised during the Depression, my mother understands thriftiness in a way that combines "use it up" care with "do without" worries. "It's hard to use the last one up," she says when we find expired cans of soup on her shelf. When I discover the last piece of bread, now moldy in the bag, or the last apple shriveled in my cupboard, I know I've inherited some "don't use it up" ideas from her. Either way, thrift is a practice that places future value on things that might be important someday. Better to take care of the possessions you have now than spend more time and money acquiring them again later when you most need them.

When I think of my grandmothers' lives, I think of the play *Trifles* written by Susan Glaspell in 1916. In *Trifles*, later published as the short story "A Jury of Her Peers," a farmwife is accused of strangling her husband while he sleeps; the wives of her accusers are asked to visit the farmhouse to gather a few things she'll need in jail. While the men search for clues to why she may have committed the murder, the women observe the "trifles" of the accused woman's life: the stinginess of the farmhouse compared to the new barn outside; a dead bird in a cage, its neck broken just like the husband's; the lack of a telephone with which to communicate with neighbors. At the end of the play, the women examine a quilt made from the tiny scraps of the jailed woman's life. When they wonder whether she was going to quilt it or knot it, the men laugh at the women's irrelevant concerns. What the men don't realize is that quilting implies the company of other women, while knotting a quilt can be accomplished alone. The women's final words to the men— "Knot it"—reveal that the men's comprehension of women's lives is "Not it"—not the knowledge they seek to convict her, knowledge the women refuse to share.

My grandmothers' lives weren't as harsh as the woman's in Glaspell's story, but they didn't have many frills for all their hard work. I've been lucky to inherit some of the "trifles" of my grandmothers' lives, traces of the ways they spent their days and the objects that they used and cherished. From Grandma Smith, I inherited a yellow Fiestaware bowl that she called her "potato salad" bowl, a cheery yellow, one of the bright colors that Fiestaware sold during the Depression. From Grandma Short, a beauty pageant winner, I inherited the rust- and black-beaded Bakelite necklace she wore when she married in a rust-colored dress with a velvet collar.

From both of my grandmothers, I have sewing notions: from Grandma Short, a round woven sewing basket, the top embellished with a long silken tassel and small Asian coins, and a box of quilt scraps that she never pieced. From Grandma Smith, a sewing machine in a simple wooden cabinet with a square stool and an amber sewing case that held her needles and fine crochet hooks. Whenever I thread a needle, I think of her advice: "Don't thread it too long or it will tangle." In other words, *don't make more work for yourself than you have to*—another lesson in economy from a woman who knew how to make the most of what she had.

A Bushel's Worth

As a child, I believed my grandparents' farms would re-main, season after season, waiting for my return, but since my grandparents died, I've only gone back once with John, our daughters, and my Colorado family to salvage what we could of the Short farmhouse before it was torn down. In rural North Dakota, abandoned farms are often used for illicit purposes like itinerant meth labs, something we wanted to avoid, so for two days we unwired Depression-era lights, unhinged pan-eled doors, unscrewed glass doorknobs, and unfastened pine moldings, rescuing what we could of our rural roots before the remains were sacrificed to the changing times.

It felt strange to be in that house without my grandparents, although their presence was everywhere, from the stove where my grandmother stood cooking to the mud porch where my grandfather processed raw milk in the stainless cream separa-tor before taking it to my uncle's creamery. More than a de-cade after my grandparents' deaths, the porch still smelled like milk. Like any abandoned house, it seemed to wait for its own-ers' return, as if they'd just gone out for a drive and would be home soon. A worn metal matchstick holder sat expectantly on the shelf next to the kitchen door. My father said I could take it if I would use it, so I slipped it in our tool bag with the hammers and crowbars. I didn't want to leave it there alone. I am using it, every time I light a fire in our woodstove.

In the bare dirt basement under the kitchen, we found a green wooden "stepback" jelly cabinet with two tall doors on the narrower top part and one latched door on the deeper bottom section. Someone, maybe Grandpa Short, had made this cabinet many years ago to hold canned goods; the paint gleamed with the soft patina called "primitive" today. Not wanting to leave it to a demolition's fate, we strapped it on top of the doors and moldings in the truck for the long trip back to Colorado.

As we left North Dakota with our load of treasures early in the morning, I watched the sun rise over the prairie as I bid farewell to my rural roots. With the long expanse of road and fields before us, new words to "Down in the Valley" played in my mind:

The green rolling prairie
The grass a foot high
The wheat fields were waving
As we said goodbye.

I haven't been back to the farms since then, except in memory each day when I smell the country air or hear a meadowlark trilling across the fields. Now those keepsakes grace the buildings at Stonebridge, transplanted reminders of my grandparents' self-sufficient lives on their land. Salvaging their farmhouses felt like desecration, but a necessary act all the same. What we left behind would have been stolen or destroyed or simply disappeared with time.

But on the farm we learn that desecration leads to resurrection. All matter is reshaped into another form. Compost becomes food for new plant growth; a rotting log sprouts mushrooms for our dinner. Each trace of those farms has become something new here, something of use to this farm in some way. The wood moldings salvaged with crowbars and hammers have been cut and mitered around windows, doors, and walls from the mudroom to the guesthouse to the Sunflower Community Room. Shelves have been fashioned from that same wood, as well as frames for photographs of the people and places we love. The old mailbox waits in the rose garden for a letter or a bird to make a home.

The doors of the old farmhouse are found throughout the many buildings of Stonebridge. One stands at the opening of the straw bale house, now used as a recording space for digital storytelling workshops. Another hangs sidewise on our kitchen wall to frame the corner where we eat. Four doors stand side by side with keyholes perfectly aligned in the Sunflower

Room to encompass the space where we gather to knit. Glass knobs and fancy doorplates too have found new lives on other doors across the farm. Two yellow lamps, their metal shades patinaed with rust, hang in the Sunflower Room, lighting our meals just as they did when my grandparents' farmhouse was new.

Inside our old farmhouse, the jelly cabinet with its green milk-paint now stands in the chatroom, so-called because we gather there with company for conversation. Inside the cabinet are other remnants of the farms—old pop bottles, glass dishes, embroidered linens, and small oil lamps with paper shades, prizes from school carnivals. An A&W mug from my Grandpa Short's dresser sits next to a jar of shell buttons saved when shirts faded and frayed. And at the back of a shelf sits a once-colorful tea tin with holes punched in the top for a grasshopper's home. I know this because I punched the holes there myself as a child and found the tin decades later in the milk house of the Smith farm before it was torn down. It is my inheritance, like the picture of my great-aunts wading in the creek with their friend from town.

Culling her collection of vintage treasures recently, my sister handed me a box of old bottles to see if I had a use for any of them. I immediately chose the Burma-Shave jar with its ribbed glass and navy blue lid. Burma-Shave was a shaving cream company whose marketing campaign placed consecutive lines of rhyming advertising jingles along highways from the 1920s to the early 60s:

Special Seats
Reserved in Hades
For Whiskered Gents
Who Scratch
The Ladies
Burma-Shave.

Every year or so, a crew would change the signs, throwing the old boards on the ground. Because the Smith farm bordered the highway, Grandpa Smith would pick up the discarded wood—still good lumber—to fix a shed or patch a broken window. My parents brought some of these signs to Colorado and now they hang in the Sunflower Room at Stonebridge. My sister had found the old Burma-Shave jar on the farm after my grandparents' deaths. It seemed fitting to reunite it with the signs advertising the shaving cream that used to fill the jar.

After I picked out some medicinal vials for bottling the berry cordial we make each fall, I noticed a small bottle with a rubber stopper for a lid. When I lifted it out of the box, I gasped. Here was Grandpa Smith's mercurochrome bottle, the one he'd used to doctor our scrapes and cuts every summer. He'd patiently lift us up to sit on the kitchen counter, the better to "paint," as he would say, our knees and elbows with the metallic orange-red tincture. Today mercurochrome is banned in the United States because it contains mercury, but back then, we believed as much in its curative powers as we did in Grandpa's doctoring skills.

Its label faded and torn, its rubber stopper hardened in the bottle's glass neck, my grandfather's mercurochrome bottle evoked another memory of childhood complaints. Mercurochrome wasn't the only medicine in the farm's kitchen cabinet. I remembered the smell of the medicine before I recalled its name: Listerine. Not the cool mint or citrus-fresh flavors of today but the antiseptic scent of the original mouthwash my grandfather used to stop our mosquito bites from itching. How we winced when that home remedy stung our arms and legs, but it kept us from scratching the mosquito bites that plagued us those hot summer nights in the North Dakota countryside. Like mercurochrome, it worked, but even if it hadn't, we wouldn't have questioned our grandfather's authority to use it. We trusted those moments of tender curing that affirmed a grandparent's love.

For years after my grandparents were gone, I took comfort in the fact that their land was still in agricultural production. But the new oil boom in what's called the Bakken formation is threatening farmland in North Dakota, a drama played out in my family as well. Today, oil wells are pumping on or nearby what were once my grandparents' farms and I am in small part a beneficiary of that oil.

My grandparents lived through the first oil boom in their region and left their mineral rights for their family's future, but they couldn't have anticipated the impact of oil production on the land. Now a neighbor worries that his farming will be curtailed because of oil, at the same time that he has wells on his own family farm. As an environmentalist, I'm worried that the extracting methods used contaminate the land and threaten the environment, but with so many in that rural community benefiting economically, it's clear the work to clean up the oil industry must be carried out on many levels, from local to global. I'm glad, though, that my grandparents didn't live to see the industrial park sprawling on acres of land across the highway from their farmhouse.

Sometimes I forget that my grandparents are no longer living and that their farmland has been sold, the farmhouses destroyed. The realization of this loss is not only sad, but frightening. If those farms are lost, then ours could be as well. What will happen when John and I are too old or ill to farm anymore? Nature's response to our absence, I'm certain, would be to return to prairie grass within a single year. But since it seems all land must be owned, I worry that the land itself will be lost to development, as has most of the farmland along the Highway 66 corridor. I'd rather have the entire ten acres return to prairie than become another overpriced housing subdivision in Boulder County. But the best outcome will be for Stonebridge to remain a small farm, so John and I will take whatever steps we can to preserve Stonebridge for future generations.

When I worry about the future of Stonebridge, I try to find reassurance in the old wisdom of the fields, the proverbs that guided my grandparents in their work: Make hay while the sun shines. Get to the root of the problem. Many hands make light work. You reap what you sow. And from Ecclesiastes: To everything there is a season and a time for every purpose under heaven.

From these words came the rhythm by which my grandparents lived their lives: Follow the daylight and the seasons. Work hard in summer while the light is long and the weather mild. Rest in winter when the days are short and the nights cold. Balance the necessary work with rest and renewal and regeneration. Each season, the land extends forgiveness and we get to start over again.

Salvaging the traces of my grandparents' farms seemed a betrayal to their way of life, like turning our backs on all they had accomplished, an admission that we would no longer be stewards of their land. But salvaging promises a continuity of their lives on *this* farm and with it, a hope that our land will remain rural.

Waste not, want not. From my grandparents, I learned to make the most of what I have. From the land at Stonebridge, I'm learning to share the most of what I'm given. With our community's support, we will do what we can to protect the land so that Stonebridge can remain a small, organic farm for the next generation of farmers. As my grandparents did before us, let us use resources wisely by following nature's generous giving, from the land to each other and back again.

When John and I made a commitment to each other, we placed our lives alongside the land at Stonebridge.

And the Earth Gives Again

Humans—despite their artistic pretensions, their sophistica-
tion, and their many accomplishments—owe their existence to a
six-inch layer of topsoil and the fact that it rains.
                    —Anonymous quote from the Fedco seed catalog

To celebrate our summer solstice anniversary, John and
I went to the big city of Denver. We like a little city
time, eating at trendy restaurants, browsing bookstores, and
swimming in the rooftop pool at our hotel while the sun sets
over the mountains. But this time, I found myself feeling more
annoyed with the incessant traffic and noise and less charmed
by urban offerings of culture and cuisine than usual. I still
loved our celebratory meal at our favorite country French
restaurant, but I was most excited when the server brought the
same kind of fava beans we grow at home.

As John and I walked around the city for a couple days, I
understood why so many city people have dogs: they have to
go outside to walk them, so at least they get a few minutes in
the relatively fresh air and sunlight every day. On the gritty
streets, I found myself seeking traces of the country: patches of
grass, pots of flowers, even farm-fresh vegetables at our meals,
anything that delivered a reprieve from cement sidewalks and
steel buildings that block the sun. Preserved from the city's
gold mining past, stone flowers and fruit embellish turn-of-
the-century buildings, their arches and columns emerging

plant-like from redstone and granite. Green floral tape twists replace fresh needles on the bare trunk of a doorway pine. Inked in a fleshy Eden between slender shoulders, a young woman grows a forest of birds and trees, the closest thing to nature I saw all weekend.

Until I heard the birds.

Birds aren't absent in the city. Pigeons and starlings huddle under eaves; robins nest in parks. But I wasn't expecting a chorus of birds as we walked down the sidewalk in the midst of a busy commercial block near the state capital, a street with more concrete and asphalt than grass or even weeds.

As John and I passed a gift shop, I heard the birds chirping loudly and in unison, as if a whole flock of birds was greeting the sun rising over a canopy of trees. Startled, I looked up above the shop's doorway for a nest. But instead I found a speaker piping out the birds' songs to the sidewalk below. Whether meant to attract customers or scare away real birds, at least their trilling muted the traffic's whine, and I smiled at the shopkeeper's ingenuity.

And then a block later, the graffiti on the side of an empty storefront asked "DO YOU FEEL REAL?" What would "real" feel like, I wondered, in a place where the natural world is so scarce that artifice supplants the real thing? Maybe urban people do know what they're missing. That's why they try to create a little bit of country in the city. I was missing it too, but I could go home again to my gardens and trees and homegrown meals. For city dwellers, tattoos would have to do.

Most urban people take six inches of topsoil and the fact that it rains for granted, at least until it's time to wash their cars. But on a farm, something happens every day to remind us that nature takes its course. Like the morning the mushroom tree broke off eight feet up from the base and toppled over to the other side of the ditch. All that decayed cottonwood, the kind that wild oyster mushrooms thrive on, had eaten the tree from the inside out. The pounds and pounds of mushrooms we'd harvested the previous two years had rotted the trunk straight through and now it would lay across the ditch until John could drag it out with the tractor and chop it into firewood. That's what happens to things in the natural world: they bloom, sprout, blossom, and ripen with new life. And then they wither, rot, decay, and decompose into the soil that will nourish the next living thing. The cycle continues, with or without us.

Like the wet snow on October 10 one year, at least two weeks before expected. Because the first frost had been unseasonably early the week before, we had already gotten as much as we could into the barn, and the moisture was helpful for the root crops. But the whole season had been strange. The late spring was so cold that we couldn't get the tomatoes, peppers, and eggplant into the field until June 7, a week later than usual, and the summer temperatures had never broken a hundred degrees. In June, talking with a member in the barn, I lamented that we'd gotten the hot weather crops out so late and worried that they'd have time to ripen. "The farmer's dilemma," she sympathized. "You can't control the weather." With a cool spring and summer, a premature first frost, and six inches of snow in early October, we had learned that lesson again.

Farmers take their best shot at each season. Our high hopes for the abundant tomatoes in the field were dashed by the early frost, but we had given our members more tomatoes than ever before. Our losses weren't devastating: we counted ourselves lucky that we hadn't gotten heavy hail—twice—like farms north of us had. Nor had we skipped a pick-up day or two because we didn't have vegetables to give. Our long-time subscribers noticed the barn was a little barer than usual in July when the second planting of beets and carrots failed, but the squashes, soft and hard, were prolific, and the onions outdid themselves for sweetness and size. Because different crops prefer different conditions—and different conditions are the one thing the weather *can* guarantee—every year parades its own

Best of Show. Each season's success cannot be foretold; sun, rain, and wind determine which vegetable will triumph.

When you live on a farm with distinct seasons like ours, your life adapts to the cycles of growth and rest. Like Pete Seeger's song "Turn, Turn, Turn," composed to words from Ecclesiastes, the farming season follows a pattern with "a time to plant" and "a time to reap," just as each day follows the sunlight in determining what can be accomplished:

> *To everything*
> *Turn, Turn, Turn*
> *There is a season*
> *Turn, Turn, Turn*
> *And a time for every purpose, under heaven.*

As the days grow shorter, so too does our work outside on the farm, and we turn toward inside pursuits. Then as the daylight increases, we turn our lives to the outside world once more. Turning and turning from inside to out, outside to in, our days and months and years pass in seasonal rhythms that become second nature because they are *based* in nature.

This sense of living within nature's cycles is part of what John and I try to teach when we work with students on our farm. We grow vegetables for an alternative high school in a mountain community above us, and each summer, host a class on farming for an interested group of students. Primarily from urban environments, the students are initially a little apprehensive about doing the "farm thing" out in the middle of nature. They arrive at the farm sleepy from their late-night habits, a little resistant to being outside so early in the day. But before they know it, they are working hard, transplanting seedlings, hoeing weeds, and harvesting the vegetables for their school's dining hall. Slowly the students learn to enjoy the lettuce, spinach, and carrots in their school's salad bar because they have grown it. One student's delight in discovering how food grows has been echoed by many young people who have worked in the Stonebridge fields: "While I was [weeding the carrots] I began to notice that the bed was going to look really good and I began to feel a really close connection between myself and the farm. The farm has taught me how to appreciate vegetables a lot more than I did before."

When we ask the students what they have enjoyed most from their time on the farm, they always say eating a vegetable straight out of the garden: they love to pull something out of the ground, wipe the soil off on their shirt (it's organic, so no worries about pesticides), and take a bite. One student said carrots reminded him of his childhood, but not because he grew up eating them: "When I was washing them, the smell of the carrots smelled so sweet and I took a bite out of the carrots. It had that perfect crunch. Sweet juices started to come out while I chewed the bright orange carrot and it still had the green part on it. It brought back memories sitting at home alone when I was just a kid, my mom working so she could put food on the table and me just sitting in front of the television watching Bugs Bunny: What's Up, Doc?"

A carrot right out of the garden—now that's what a carrot should taste like. Farming gives these students two gifts: the gift of a carrot right out of the ground and the gift of the knowledge that you can eat a carrot that way. I've had my own spiritual experiences with carrots at about 10:30 on a Saturday morning when I need a little something to keep me going until the pick is finished. It's been a long time since breakfast, I'm hungry, and I've got a carrot in my hand. What else would I do but eat it? That's why we grew it, after all.

We can all learn lessons from the earth if we pay attention to its insistent wisdom. Aldo Leopold's *A Sand County Almanac*, like other classic nature writings such as *Desert Solitaire* by Edward Abbey and *Refuge* by Terry Tempest Williams, combines exquisite detail of his corner of the natural world with an urgent appeal for protecting that world—if it's not already too late. First published in 1949, *Sand County* is arranged by months; the February chapter is particularly apt for Stonebridge:

There are two spiritual dangers in not owning a farm. One is the danger of supposing that breakfast comes from the grocery, and the other that heat comes from the furnace.

To avoid the first danger, one should plant a garden, preferably where there is no grocer to confuse the issue.

To avoid the second, he should lay a split of good oak on the andirons, preferably where there is no furnace, and let it warm his shins while a February blizzard tosses the trees outside. If one has cut, split, hauled, and piled his own oak, and let his mind work the while, he will remember much about where the heat comes from, and with a wealth of detail denied to those who spend the week end in town astride a radiator.

Here on the Front Range, winter eventually catches up with us. New Year's Eve is cold and snowy and snowstorms come in waves, diminishing in power but keeping the landscape softly blanketed in white. The nights are frigid, but in the house, we're warmed by a wood fire, one provided by nature and by John with his chainsaw and his willingness to go outside first thing in the morning for wood. Many years ago, our hot water heating system went on the blink. We were using the woodstove pretty regularly already because we liked the warmth it gave, reaching further into corners than less powerful heat. When the furnace went out, we decided to go all the way with wood.

Or almost all the way. The ceiling-high windows on the south side of the farmhouse provide passive solar heat and we have a couple space heaters for our offices or to warm the cast-iron tub in the bathroom. Primarily, though, the woodstove does the job.

Each year since we let the furnace go, we've made some improvements. Because the farmhouse is one hundred years old, we had extra insulation blown into the walls. What a difference that made, mostly to keep in the heat from the woodstove rather than lose it out the wood walls. Next, we built a wood hut to keep the logs dry and handy outside the back door. Designed by John Bell with a scavenged satellite dish for a roof, it makes trips to the woodpile much more pleasant, even in the snow. We've lined and improved the old chimney and have it cleaned periodically by a chimney sweep. We also bought, at our friend Peter's advice, a colored temperature gauge so we could monitor the optimum flame. Yellow is too low; red is too high. We like to keep it "in the mustard," we say, where the wood burns most efficiently.

The biggest improvement is the wood itself from the trees growing along the three irrigation ditches. For years we burned cottonwood, since it was the most common, but that wood burns like toilet paper—lots of ash, not much heat. Now we're burning willow, apple, and Russian olive, the latter a weed tree that John has sworn to rid from our land.

I'm glad John doesn't mind swinging an axe as he's "let[ting] his mind work the while." And I'm glad to hear the "thump" in the woodbox in the morning as he drops a load of dry logs for the first fire of the day. It's good to know where our heat comes from, as well as our food. Leopold would approve.

One winter evening, John and I came home from a mountain drive to find this message on our answering machine: "Hi. This is your neighbor. If you're home today between two and four, give me a call." We recognized our neighbor Lois's voice, but it was too late to call by the time we got the message. Wondering if everything was all right, we speculated about the call. Had she seen John's letter to the editor accusing the cement company across the highway of being a bad neighbor by contaminating our air and water and was she calling to agree? Had our goat gotten into her yard again and stripped her trees of their bark? Was she calling about her granddaughter, best friends with our youngest daughter? Hoping for the best, we went to bed.

First thing the next morning, we found out the real reason for the call: Lois wanted to bring us a loaf of freshly baked bread. She was baking again that very afternoon and would call when she took it out of the oven. Later that day the three of us devoured half the loaf with hot tea as we strategized clean air campaigns, errant goats, the friendship of daughters and granddaughters, and saving the world from itself.

I thought about what a wonderful gift we'd been given. Not just a loaf of bread, but a seventy-year-old neighbor who is as compassionate as she is wise. I wondered what we had done to deserve such an unexpected gift. Spontaneous and unanticipated, such gifts are all the more precious in their offering. Only nature's grace and the power of community, I decided, could explain our fortune.

Working in the flower garden one late summer day, I hear a pack of young coyotes yipping on the other side of the Highland ditch that borders the eastern edge of our farm. I've heard them there before and wonder whether a mother coyote makes a den there for her pups. I'm heartened to hear their playful yapping and know they're still around. We haven't domesticated the farm so much that coyotes can't play along the ditch banks or run across the meadow.

This summer on one of our mountain day hikes, John and I heard the wail of a siren rising from the valley far below where the highway leads to the pass. It reminded us that even on a mountainside, we aren't that far from civilization. Then, like a call and response, a lone coyote answered the siren's cry with a plaintive howl. Back and forth, machine and animal, they sang until the vehicle was too far down the highway to answer any longer. With one last howl, the coyote said good-bye. Or perhaps good riddance to an interloper disturbing the mountain's peace.

In 1851, when Thoreau wrote, "In wildness is the preservation of the world," he raised an alarm for a wilderness already diminished by human encroachment. In the ensuing years, his warning has become ever more urgent as the danger comes in ways Thoreau could never have imagined, through devastation of the climate in which the earth and its habitants survive. In the midst of shrinking wilderness and mounting climate crises, the loss of the cultivated spaces we call farmland is also cause for alarm and action. As more of these spaces disappear to development and urbanization, the push to turn remaining land toward industrial farming's chemical and oil dependency grows with its false promise of efficiency. It may be too late to reclaim much of the cultivated space of my grandparents' time, but the success of small farms like ours can help us rethink how food can and should be grown. We must preserve the places that still exist—from open space lands to small acreages to abandoned urban lots to backyards—for the cultivation of food we will need in the future.

In his 1995 essay "Conserving Communities," agricultural activist Wendell Berry warned of the conflict between local farming traditions and corporate agricultural interests: "In their dealings with the countryside and its people, the promoters of the so-called global economy . . . believe that a farm or a forest is or ought to be the same as a factory [and] that the nature or ecology of any given place is irrelevant to the use of it." Only our stewardship prevents the disappearance of farmland into intractable development—acres and acres of monochromatic residential, commercial and industrial tracts that scrape, fumigate, and obliterate the natural world.

Wilderness needs protection, true, but farmland needs our protection too. The bumper sticker on our car reads "Know Farmers Know Food," yet the homonym is more urgently true: NO FARMERS, NO FOOD. Food comes first from the earth, not a factory or store. If we fail to preserve land for agricultural production, if we depend on multinational corporations to provide our food, and if we continue to replace organic and natural food with chemically produced and processed food products, we will create the conditions of our own demise.

In November 2008, when the US economy began to falter dramatically, Miller Farms, a six-hundred-acre, multi-generation family farm north of Denver, invited the public to glean potatoes, carrots, beets, and onions left in the fields after the farm's official season was over. The farmers expected five to ten thousand people to take them up on their offer over the weekend. They were shocked when 40,000 showed up and the food was gone from the fields in an hour. Many of the gleaners came without any farm tools and tried to dig with a screwdriver or windshield wiper from their car instead. As a Denver newspaper reported, people were appreciative of the free food and the farmers were especially happy that children were learning where food comes from. "Teach them where potatoes come from—the ground," Joe Miller said. "Not a tree, not out of a plastic bag, not out of a greenhouse."

The value of family farms like this cannot be measured in mere dollars and cents. Preserving agricultural land for local food production ensures food security for our children and grandchildren, a value that is overlooked by agricultural policies that privilege short-term profits. The vision of the local food movement is to ring each community with CSAs and small market farmers who provide the majority of a community's fresh food needs.

As each area creates its own food system, eating habits will adapt to the availability of seasonal foods. As our members know, spring in the Front Range of the Rocky Mountains means spinach that revitalizes our bodies after a long winter, while fall means squash and roots that prepare our bodies for the coming cold. Eating locally-produced foods in season connects us to the cycles of the natural world and reminds us that food is grown, not just sold, a lesson we must take to heart if we are to protect the health of the earth—and our own. Barbara Kingsolver's *Animal, Vegetable, Miracle: A Year of Food Life* details how her family's life was transformed by eating locally, both from their own garden and animals and from the work of other farmers. Although she realizes that growing for a livelihood has "a whole set of different chores and worries" than growing for one family, like others in the local food movement she experiences the benefits of health, environment, and delicious eating all the same, discovering for herself "some element of farm nostalgia in our family past, real or imagined: a secret longing for some connection to a life where a rooster crows in the yard."

In a challenge to industrial agriculture, this country is witnessing a resurgence of small-scale farming, both because of the development of a new local idea of economy and because large-scale agribusinesses are proving unsustainable in many ways. In 2007, Stonebridge was the sixty-sixth farm to register on the Local Harvest web site of small-scale organic producers and just two years later, twenty thousand farms were listed there. John and I are encouraged by the new farmers springing up in our region and we have mentored several dedicated and skillful enthusiasts who want to make a living—and a life— around the land.

Without grandparents and their farms to teach us how to be farmers, we have turned to each other for the knowledge we need. Still, I worry about the disappearance of old time family farming. I worry that experts like Harvey Nelsen, who sells and repairs and knows more about tractors than anyone else, can't be replaced by a new generation of mechanics because Harvey is more than a mechanic. He's a part of living history from a time when most every family had a tractor.

When our tiller seized up and quit running one day, John called Harvey to ask him what to do. "Well, have you been checking the gear oil?" Harvey asked. John admitted he hadn't realized it needed oil and had been running it for years without adding any to the reservoir. "Well, a guy could take out the bearing and replace it," Harvey suggested in his inimitable "a guy could" way. And how might a guy get it out? John wondered. "Well, you just pull it out or you get a puller," Harvey replied. I could hear the patience in his voice at John's many questions. Harvey's always patient and he always helps. What would we do without his kindness and expertise? What will we do when Harvey closes shop?

Farming is risky business, but so is love. I might have been a city girl all my life if a farm—and a farmer—hadn't come along. But if I hadn't spent my first years and my childhood summers on my grandparents' farms, would a farmer and a farm have been the choice I made? I don't think so.

When we choose one person to love, we pretend that our time together is infinite. We plan for a mutual future and hope that with love in our hearts, we'll see each other through.

When we choose one place to love, we must remember that the land will succeed our earthly lives. The earth has its own sense of time, one measured by rotations rather than devices, but in what shape it will survive is not assured. To preserve a place we love, we must admit our human impermanence and extend our efforts to a time beyond our own measure. We must plan for the land to go on without us, hoping that the legacy of our stewardship will continue for as long as humans inhabit the earth.

When John and I made a commitment to each other, we placed our lives alongside the land at Stonebridge. We care about this ten acres of land and each other as part of caring for the world around us. We've faced our own environmental struggles here. With like-minded community members, we met and marched for years to prevent a nearby multinational cement company from burning tires in their outdated kiln— and won. We opposed the use of genetically modified seeds on county open space land leased to conventional farmers—and lost. But we'll continue to work for this land and for the production, distribution, and celebration of locally grown food because when we do, a vaster web of life is sustained, from the soil that nurtures the seeds to the bees that pollinate the plants to the people whose lives are enriched in immeasurable ways. Capricious weather, a warming climate, and the vagaries of public whim make farming an unpredictable business, but like love, it's a risk we're willing to take.

Wendell Berry's *The Unsettling of America* draws a provocative connection between our social and environmental actions: "[I]t is impossible to care for each other more or differently than we care for the earth." The earth teaches us that abundance must be shared without hesitation or pause, a verdant generosity that never asks, "How much?" but instead reminds, "For all." When we give the gift of each other, we are practicing what we learn from the earth's bounty: giving more than is needed, without reserve or expectation of return, from the deepest part of our hearts.

We work. We wait. And the earth gives again. Each Stonebridge morning, we think about what comes next. We plan our days, our weeks, our years, and our lives around the land. We may not accomplish everything we set out to do, but we always accomplish more than we ever thought we could. To water, soil, air, and sun, we owe our existence. To the community that supports us, we owe our thanks. To the land that sustains us, we owe our lives. We have so much. We have learned from the earth that when we practice gratitude, not greed, we will have plenty and plenty more to come.

Acknowledgments

From seed to harvest, many generous hands have tended this work. The author extends her deepest gratitude

To Torrey House Press, for recognizing that the West has stories too.

To the Stonebridge community, for knowing what "share" means.

To Sian, Carol, Andrea, Patty, Lorna, and Kari, for reading, writing, and believing.

To Dad, for navigating between North Dakota and Colorado.

To Mom, for cooking for threshers.

To Ariane, from the start.

To Collin, for the future.

And to John. You are my summer, fall, winter, and spring.

Additional Readings

The following works are mentioned in *A Bushel's Worth:*

Abbey, Edward. *Desert Solitaire: A Season in Wilderness.* New York: Ballantine, 1968.

Berry, Wendell. "Conserving Communities" in *Another Turn of the Crank.* Washington, DC: Counterpoint, 1995.

Berry, Wendell. *The Unsettling of America: Culture and Agriculture.* San Francisco: Sierra Club Books, 1996.

Beston, Henry. *The Outermost House: A Year of Life on the Great Beach of Cape Cod.* New York: Henry Holt and Company, 1928.

Glaspell, Susan. *"Trifles"* in *The Norton Anthology of Literature by Women: The Tradition in English.* Edited by Sandra M. Gilbert and Susan Gubar. New York: Norton, 1985.

Harris, Joanne. *Blackberry Wine.* New York: Harper Collins Perennial, 2000.

Henderson, Elizabeth and Robyn Van En. *Sharing the Harvest: A Guide to Community-Supported Agriculture.* White River Junction, Vermont: Chelsea Green Publishing, 1999.

Hudson, Lois Phillips. *The Bones of Plenty.* Boston: Little, Brown and Company, 1962.

Kingsolver, Barbara, Steven L. Hopp, and Camille Kingsolver. *Animal, Vegetable, Miracle: A Year of Food Life.* New York: HarperCollins, 2007.

Leopold, Aldo. *A Sand County Almanac.* New York: Ballantine, 1949.

LeSueur, Meridel. "Harvest" in *Late Harvest: Rural American Writing*. Edited by David R. Pichaske. New York: Smithmark, 1996.

Nestle, Joan. *Food Politics: How the Food Industry Influences Nutrition and Food*. Berkeley: University of California Press, 2002.

Rilke, Rainier Marie. "The Apple Orchard" in *Rainier Marie Rilke: Selected Poems*. Translated by Albert Ernest Flemming. London: Routledge & Kegan Paul, 1986.

Robertson, Adele Crockett. *The Orchard: A Memoir*. New York: Bantam, 1995.

Sackville-West, Vita. *In Your Garden*. London: Frances Lincoln Ltd, 1951.

Spaid, Gregory. *Grace: Photographs of Rural America*. New London, New Hampshire: Safe Harbor Books, 2000.

Thoreau, Henry David. *Walden; Or, Life in the Woods*. Boston: Houghton Mifflin,1906.

Thoreau, Henry David. "Walking." *The Atlantic Monthly* (June, 1862).

Walker, Alice. "In Search of Our Mothers' Gardens." In *In Search of Our Mothers' Gardens*. San Diego: Harvest HBJ, 1984.

Williams, Terry Tempest. *Refuge: An Unnatural History of Family and Place*. New York: Vintage, 1991, 2001.

Woolf, Virginia. *To the Lighthouse*. Orlando: Harcourt, 1927.

About Torrey House Press

*The economy is a wholly owned subsidiary of the environment,
not the other way around.*
—Senator Gaylord Nelson, founder of Earth Day

Headquartered in Salt Lake City and Torrey, Utah, Torrey House Press is an independent book publisher of literary fiction and creative nonfiction about the environment, people, cultures, and resource management issues relating to America's wild places. Torrey House Press endeavors to increase awareness of and appreciation for the importance of natural landscape through the power of pen and story.

2% for the West is a trademark of Torrey House Press designating that two percent of Torrey House Press sales are donated to a select group of not-for-profit environmental organizations in the West and used to create a scholarship available to up-and-coming writers at colleges throughout the West.

Torrey House Press
www.torreyhouse.com

See www.torreyhouse.com for our thought-provoking discussion guide for *A Bushel's Worth: An Ecobiography*.

Also Available from Torrey House Press

Evolved: Chronicles of a Pleistocene Mind
by Maximilian Werner
With startling insights, Werner explores how our Pleistocene instincts inform our everyday decisions and behaviors in this modern day Walden.

The Legend's Daughter
by David Kranes
These fast-paced stories set in contemporary Idaho explore intricate dynamics between fathers and sons, unlikely friends, people and place.

Grind
by Mark Maynard
The gritty realism of Hemingway joins the irreverence of Edward Abbey in these linked short stories set in and around Reno, Nevada.

The Ordinary Truth
by Jana Richman
Today's western water wars and one family's secrets divide three generations of women as urban and rural values collide.

Recapture
by Erica Olsen
This captivating short story collection explores the canyons, gulches, and vast plains of memory along with the colorful landscapes of the West.

Tributary
by Barbara K. Richardson
A courageous young woman flees polygamy in 1860s Utah, but finds herself drawn back to the landscapes that shaped her.

The Scholar of Moab
by Steven L. Peck
Philosophy meets satire, poetry, cosmology, and absurdity in this tragicomic brew of magical realism and rural Mormon Utah.

The Plume Hunter
by Renée Thompson
Love and lives are lost amid conflict over killing wild birds for women's hats in Oregon and California in the late nineteenth century.

Crooked Creek
by Maximilian Werner
Blood Meridian finds *A Farewell to Arms* in this short and beautiful novel set in 1890s Utah.